Stéphanie Deméry

THE TRADITIONAL «CUISINE PROVENÇALE»

Preface by Frederic Dard

Rivages

ISBN : 2-903059-29-2

To Charles

Preface

They say God created the world in six days.
They say that on the seventh day, He rested.
Personally, I think He spent his Sunday playing, loving, perfecting Provence.
There is an old french saying : Besides men there are englishmen.
So I like to say : there is France and there is Provence.
Provence with its Mistral wind, Provence bursting with flowers, cypress trees,
cantaloups, noisy cicadas and above all the sun.
And after all, Provence is the only one of our provinces that relishes the subtle
redolence of garlic.
The only way to know a country is through its cuisine. It is the rustling
essence of the land. Somehow our soul is tested through a griddle and the
sensual enjoyment goes to our heart rather than our body.
Stephanie Deméry, an authentic « provençale », has made an important book.
I suspect she wrote it with a rosemary twig dipped in olive oil, a clove of
garlic as an eraser. If only for the bewitching use of words, this book should
have the star place on your spice shelf.
The true spirit of provençal cuisine, the soul of it, is within these pages.
And how wittily this book is offered to us ! Quick, precise and efficient it
brings you one of the most pleasant and certainly one of the best cuisines in
the world within the reach of your fork.
Even if your grandmother was from the north of the country rather than
from Provence, and your sweet aunt from Brittany and not from Camargue,
you will learn to create those dishes. They are, I confess, the secret motive for
our provençal escapades. Leafing through this book, the heady fantasy of
sitting on a terrace shaded by rustling sycamores already will taunt you.
Reading this book, you will welcome the pervasive enchantment of Provence
on your plate. Using this book you will become the little brother of our
famous provençal poet Mistral.
But let's listen to Stephanie Deméry :
« Once upon a time there was garlic, there was olive oil and « la farigoule »...
All of her recipes remind me of another glorious provençal writer, Alphonse
Daudet.

Frédéric Dard

Contents

Olive oil, Garlic and Aromatic herbs

Olive oil

There cannot be good cuisine without the fruity, fragrant olive oil.

« Today, the exceptional health value of olive oil has been aknowledged, and for this reason it should be used as a primary source of nutrition ». So says Professor Charbonnier, General Secretary to the French Hepatology Association.

The olive oil which I use for all my cooking is pressed by the Oleicole Cooperative of Maussane-les-Alpilles. Here is its story :

The oil mill of the Oleicole Cooperative from the Baux Valley, in Maussane-les-Alpilles was built between 1600 - 1620, under the consecutive reigns of Henry IV and Louis XIII. At that time, agriculture, protected by Sully (then Prime Minister for Henry IV), was not exactly the country's poor relation, and France must have been rich indeed, to be able to build such elaborate constructions, when you realize that there were at least 20 of these oil mills in the country of Les Baux, three hamlets today known as Maussane, Mouriès and le Paradou.

The oil mill of Maussane was erected by the Lord of Manville. It had an adjacent flour mill. The original mill was just a vaulted construction, the additions were built in 1616. Nested in the walls you can see the two sites used to house three presses each. In the two arches facing them, there were two grinding wheels. The grinding wheels were rotated by the horses and serviced two presses.

A pile of « cabas » (sacks) was placed in the press. Approximately 40-50 cabas provided 50 kilos of olive paste. Each cabas was stacked, one upon the other, then doused with several liters of boiling water. The pressure on the sacks was very light, maybe 50-60 kilograms per square inch. The hot water was used solely to help release the oil.

Two presses were a « ban », and the production was evaluated by the liters produced for each ban.

The cabas, also called « escourtins », were made of braiden straw (jonc). The peasant women wove them during most of the summer.

There were six workers per mill : le Baile, the oil trieur, the horseman (charretier), and three hands.

When the press was assembled one of the workers adjusted the « small barre ». When the pressure diminished, the « baron » was added and the « charretier » aided the three hands in their efforts. For the final pressing, the « grande barre » was used, le Baile helped the oil trieur and the four others.

The oil was stored in vats of 200-400 liters, in a place called the « l'estive ». This room was half-buried in the ground, so as to insure a stable temperature all the year round.

Today, the procedure is the same, but of course, everything is mechanized, and the quality of the oil is better since the olive paste is pressed cold, without any water, and the oil is almost never in contact with the water of the olives. There are no special formula for making good olive oil. Mainly, one must use the finest fresh olives, and keep the equipment, the vats and the mill impeccably clean.

Garlic

Garlic is regarded as one the oldest medicinal and aromatic plants throughout the world. It was cultivated by the Egyptians ; the Greeks could not stand it, but the Romans were very fond of it and they brought it to Provence.
It is used generously in the seasoning of pork, lamb, poultry, rabbits, sauces (huge quantity in aioli), soups and salads.
Garlic also contains undeniable medecinal values ; it is the most potent remedies against worms.
It is used fresh, in cloves.
Boiled garlic retains all of its properties but you should not use it with hot oil as it becomes acrid.
If you are upset by its strong flavor, you can get rid of it by drinking milk or chewing fresh parsley leaves.

Aromatic herbs

Herbs bring sun to our cuisine. They are a must as they add a delicate, agreable zest to most dishes.
These are the most used in provençal cooking.

Thyme

Fresh or dry, it is a must. It is perfect for long braising or stewing. In small quantity, it perfumes a roast lamb, a marinade for red meats and it is indispensable on all grilled meats.
Thyme is always used in a "bouquet garni".
You should use it alone or mixed with parsley, garlic, onions or bay leaves, but never use it with marjoram.
Dry thyme is much stronger than fresh thyme.

Chervil

The subtle, anis like scent of chervil is lost in cooking. It should be used only at the last moment to sprinkle hot dishes such as omelets, vegetables and poultry.
You can also use it in salad dressing and on all grilled meats.
A good idea to be served with « apéritif » : sprinkle it, finely minced, on small buttered toasts. It's delicious.

Basil

This is one the royal herbs of Provence.
It enhances all vegetables, raw or cooked, and is exceptionally perfect with tomatoes.
A basic sauce of basil mixed with olive oil is delicious with fish or pasta.
Always try to use fresh leaves, they are marvellous in salads and mayonnaise.
Basil can be mixed with garlic, onions, sage, rosemary, thyme and tarragon.

Aromatic herbs

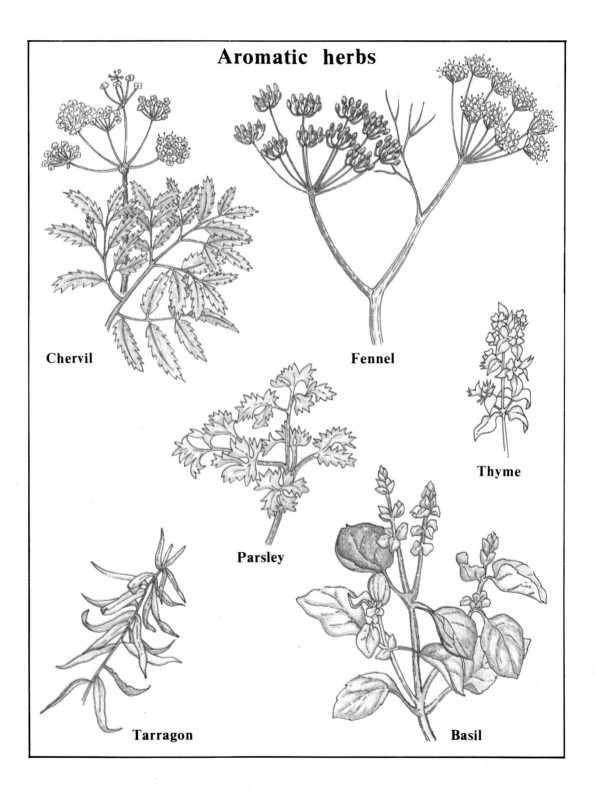

Chervil

Fennel

Thyme

Parsley

Tarragon

Basil

Fennel

Fennel has featherlike leaves ; it also has an aniseed taste. The leaves should always be used fresh, but the twigs and seeds dried, are used in fish soup and grilled fish.
Fresh, it enhances the flavor of salads and makes a very delicate cold flavored butter.

Bay leaf

You can use both the bay leaves or the berries. They can be fresh or dry.
They flavor all stews, marinades and tomatoes sauces.
They should always be crumbled or crushed.
In shish-kebab, you can alternate fresh leaves, pieces of meat and vegetables.
Bay leaves are always part of a "bouquet garni".
Add at the beginning of cooking.

Mint

Very refreshing, mint leaves should always be used fresh.
When minced they enhance the flavor of steamed vegetables.
Can also be added to forcemeats and to our proverbial cream and cottage cheese (fromage blanc).

Parsley

Flat leaf parsley, also known as italian parsley has more flavor than the curly leaf variety.
Delightful with cottage or cream cheese, it is at its best with all egg dishes.
It is a must for "bouquets garnis", and all freshly minced herbs. (Fines Herbs).
You can season almost every dish with it, omelets, fish, grilled meats, stews, salads etc...
A hash of freshly minced parsley and garlic will add an extra zest to most of your meat dishes when sprinkled or added at the last moment.

Aromatic herbs

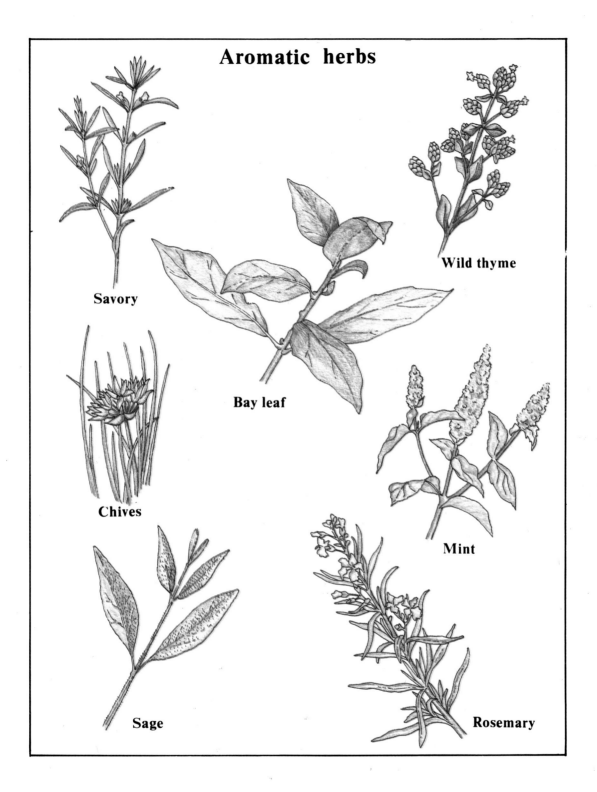

Savory

Wild thyme

Bay leaf

Chives

Mint

Sage

Rosemary

Tarragon

The leaves should always be used fresh. They add a delicate flavor to all bechamel sauces served with white meats ; they are wonderful in wine vinegar, poultry, forcemeat, minced meats, marinade, soups, cold flavored butter, poached fish, omelettes as well as with asparagus and salads.
Tarragon is also delicious minced with fresh chives and chervil, blended with cream cheese or cottage cheese.
But you should use it with moderation (particularly when mixed with other herbs) because its flavor can be overpowering. It is most succulent with shallot.

Sage

Sage also has a very potent flavor. It should always be used fresh and with discretion. It is traditional in forcemeat when stuffing poultry, pork dishes or veal.
It flavors sausage meat and mixed with cottage cheese, makes a very good stuffing for raviolis.
It has a strong and bitter flavor but mixes well with onions and garlic.
Use sparingly.

Savory

It is in the spring that the young leaves of the savory are at there most pungent. Fresh or dried, they are used on scrambled eggs, stews, beans etc...
Do not add before the cooking is almost finished.

Chives

This herbs is well known to all european cuisines. Finely minced, you should sprinkle it at the last moment on dishes such as soups, potatoes, raw or cooked vegetables and salads.

Wild thyme (serpolet)

Wild thyme is much praised in all the mediterranean countries. It is very similar to thyme and as such, is recommended for all dishes that are heavy to digest. The taste is bitter and spicy and can bring memories of hot sunny days by a sandy beach.

Rosemary

Rosemary leaves have a very strong taste. A small leaf or a twig inside a chicken can permeate the whole bird. Use it sparingly, with lamb, pork, poultry, potatoes and in marinade.
You can also stuff some rosemary into fish to be grilled.

Soups

Aïgo Boulido
Soup of boiled garlic

For six persons :
- *5 to 6 cloves of garlic,*
- *2 to 3 leaves of sage,*
- *2 bay leaves,*
- *1 sprig of thyme,*
- *1 quart of water,*
- *olive oil,*
- *salt and pepper,*
- *toasts, cut into triangles, or grilled slices of French bread.*

This soup is the answer to yesterday's binge.

Peel the cloves of garlic, crush them or cut them in four. Add to the quart of water, along with the sage, the bay leaves, the sprig of thyme, salt and pepper.

In a saucepan, bring all of the ingredients to a boil for 10 to 15 minutes.

Remove the herbs before serving the broth. You may leave the garlic in, as it is very digestible.

You can serve this broth as it is, or over slices of grilled bread, with olive oil added.

Boiled garlic is the best way to clear one's head.

Soupe à l'aïl
Garlic soup

For six persons :
- *1 ½ quarts of water,*
- *5 to 6 cloves of garlic,*
- *3 ½ ounces of thin vermicelli,*
- *1 tablespoon of olive oil,*
- *2 egg yolks,*
- *1 bay leaf,*
- *6 slices of stale bread,*
- *1 cup of grated cheese (Swiss is recommended),*
- *salt and pepper.*

Peel the garlic and crush in a mortar. If you do not have a mortar, use a garlic press, or the flat part of the blade of a large knife.

Put the bay leaf, the crushed garlic, the 1 ½ quarts of water, the salt and pepper into a 3 quarts saucepan. Bring to a boil, then throw in the vermicelli. Bring to a boil again, then lower the fire and cook for 5 more minutes, stirring. Remove from fire.

In a soup tureen, beat the egg yolks with a wooden spoon, then, still beating, add the soup in a thin stream. This way the eggs will not curdle and the soup will thicken.

Correct the seasoning.

Serve hot on slices of stale bread, with Swiss cheese.

Soupe de poisson
Fish soup

The best way to make this fish soup a success, is to use what we call « rock fish » from the Mediterranean Sea. (This soup has nothing to do with the famous Bouillabaisse). Since it is really impossible to find those fish in any other climate, here are some good substitutions : Conger Eels, Red Snapper, Sea Bass, Flounder, Sea Trout, Grouper, Porgy, or Halibut.

To prepare fish for cooking, have them cleaned and scaled. Cut them in slices or cubes. The crabs you can use are blue-clawed crabs or Maryland crabs.

For six persons :
- *2 pounds of fish,*
- *24 little crabs or 12 blue-clawed,*
- *5 tablespoons of olive oil*
- *2 cloves of garlic, crushed,*
- *2 tomatoes,*
- *2 quarts of water,*
- *1 cup of rouille (see recipe p. 122),*
- *1 white onion, minced,*
- *1 leek (use only the white section),*
- *1 sprig of fennel, 1 of savory and 2 bay leaves,*
- *2 to 3 pinches of saffron,*
- *12 small garlic toasts (rubbed with garlic),*
- *salt and pepper.*

Pour the olive oil into a soup kettle and sautée the minced onion, the white of the leek, the crushed garlic, the tomatoes (roughly cut), the twig of fennel, the savory, and the bay leaves, until tender but not brown.

Add the fish and the crabs. Add salt and pepper and fry on a medium fire until the fish becomes a beautiful golden color.

Then add 2 quarts of water and let boil for 15 minutes.

Take out the crabs and pass the fish through a sieve, or purée it through a food processor or food mill.

Return this mash to the kettle and correct the seasoning as this soup should be quite spicy.

Add two or three pinches of saffran. Bring to a boil. Serve the soup very hot with grated Swiss cheese, garlic toasts and rouille.

Soupe au pistou
Pistou

For six persons :
- *2 pounds of small string beans,*
- *1 pound of fresh white beans,*
- *½ pound of fresh kidney beans*
  (If you cannot find fresh beans, use dry beans. Reduce the measurement by half and soak overnight),
- *2 zuccini,*
- *4 carrots,*
- *2 potatoes,*
- *1 onion,*
- *5 ounces of large pasta (Macaroni, for example).*

Pistou sauce :
- *1 tomato,*
- *3 cloves of garlic,*
- *1 small bunch of fresh basil,*
- *3 tablespoons of olive oil,*
- *grated Swiss cheese,*
- *salt and pepper.*

First, prepare the string beans by cutting them in small pieces.

Shell the white and kidney beans, or strain them if dry beans were used.

Dice the zuccini - Peel and dice the carrots, potatoes and the onions.

In a soup kettle (6 quarts) add all of the vegetables and cover with cold water. Add salt and pepper. Simmer for approximately 40 minutes.

Approximately 15 minutes before serving, add the paste.

As the soup is cooking prepare the pistou sauce : Peel and crush the garlic cloves in a mortar, adding the basil leaves (which have been minced). Mix well to form a paste. Add the tomato, peeled and cut, and mix again. Little by little, pour in the olive oil. You should have a well-blended paste. Ladle about a cup of the broth from the soup kettle and add to the paste. Mix well.

Reserve the sauce.

Serve the soup. Everyone should add his own quantity of pistou sauce, as he/she desires. Then spinkle with grated Swiss cheese.

Pistou soup is one of the jewels of the cuisine of Provence. It is usually served on hot summer nights.

Salads and Vegetables

Salade « Gardianne »
« Gardianne » salad

For six persons :
- *3 large potatoes,*
- *1 apple (Golden Delicious, if possible),*
- *2 tablespoons of pastis (Ricard or Pernod),*
- *1 celery heart, fresh,*
- *6 ounces of short grain rice,*
- *2 tablespoons of fresh tarragon leaves,*
- *4 generous tablespoons of olive oil,*
- *1 teaspoon of white cider vinegar,*
- *salt and pepper.*

Peel and cut the potatoes into small cubes. Cook them in a large pan. Do not overcook ; they should stay firm.

Peel the apple and cut also into small cubes.

Mix the cooked potatoes and the diced apple in a salad bowl and pour the pastis over them. Let stand for about one hour.

Cut the celery heart into cubes also, and add to the salad bowl.

Cook the rice, rinse with cold water, drain well and add to the salad mixture, mixing thoroughly.

Prepare the dressing with the olive oil, the vinegar, salt and pepper, and the tarragon leaves, which have been chiseled beforehand.

Pour the dressing over the salad and toss well.

Refrigerate and serve very cold.

Pastis : An anis scented alcool, traditional in Provence.
Gardianne : In Camargue, they raise bulls, mostly for bull-fight. The gardians ares the cow-boys of Camargue.

Salade fraîcheur
Fresh summer salad

For six persons :
- *2 large bunches of parsley,*
- *1 heart of lettuce (Boston or bibb) cut into thin ribbons,*
- *1 bunch of fresh mint, freshly chiseled,*
- *2 small white onions,*
- *3 medium tomatoes,*
- *3 lemons,*
- *4 ounces of short grain rice,*
- *4 generous tablespoons of olive oil,*
- *salt and pepper.*

Cook the rice in salted water for approximately 15 minutes. It should stay firm.

Chisel very finely the lettuce heart, the mint, the parsley, and the white onions.

Peel and seed the tomatoes, then cut them into tiny cubes.

Mix the ingredients in a salad bowl.

Make a dressing with the olive oil, the lemons, the salt and the pepper.

Keep refrigerated, and correct seasoning before serving.

Salades de légumes grillés
Salad of grilled vegetables

For six persons :
- *5 red peppers,*
- *5 green peppers,*
- *5 small eggplants,*
- *5 zuccini,*
- *½ cup of olive oil (at least),*
- *2 cloves of garlic,*
- *parsley and chives,*
- *salt and pepper*

Small, tender vegetables are best for this salad.

Open and seed the red and green peppers. Roast them under the grill of a very hot oven. Then remove the skin (it should come off easily). Cut the peppers into fine strips. Reserve on a platter. Slice the eggplants and the zuccini in thin strips sprinkle with olive oil, salt and pepper.

Roast them in a very hot oven.

Crush the garlic. Mince the parsley and chives. Mix the garlic and the minced herbs with the rest of the olive oil. Salt and pepper.

In a flat dish, layer the vegetables and pour the oil-herb dressing over them.

Refrigerate and eat cold.

Salade à la tapenado
Salad with tapenado

For six persons :
- *1 pound of small red potatoes,*
- *1 pound of red plum tomatoes,*
- *½ pound of white onions,*
- *¼ pound of black olives (use only olives cured in oil),*
- *2 large tablespoons of minced parsley,*
- *6 tablespoons of olive oil,*
- *1 tablespoon of vinegar,*
- *2 tablespoons of tapenado (see recipe, p. 121),*
- *2 cloves of garlic, crushed,*
- *salt and pepper.*

Cook the peeled potatoes on medium heat 15 to 20 minutes. Let cool.

When they are cold, cut them into medium slices.

Quarter the tomatoes. Thinly slice the onions. Mix both in a salad bowl.

In another mixing bowl, prepare the dressing, thinning the tapenado with the olive oil, the crushed garlic, the vinegar, and the parsley. Correct seasoning. When ready to serve, add the dressing and the black olives to the salad.

Anchoïade

For six persons : • *12 fresh or salted fillets of anchovies,*
• *2 cups of olive oil,*
• *¾ cup of vinegar.*

Rinse the anchovies under cold water.

Line them in a terra cotta or enamel pot. Pour in the olive oil and the vinegar.

Very slowly cook the anchovies until they form a paste, well-mixed with the olive oil.

Let cool and serve as garnish for fresh, raw vegetables such as cardons, celery hearts, very small white onions, small purple artichokes, tomatoes, etc. Also hard-boiled eggs.

This paste may be kept in a covered glass or china jar, in the refrigerator for at least 2 months.

Artichauts à la barigoulo
Artichokes barigoulo style

For six persons :
- *12 beautiful purple artichokes (small),*
- *2 white onions, minced,*
- *¾ pound of white mushrooms, minced,*
- *2 cups of olive oil,*
- *5 tablespoons of dry white wine,*
- *1 tablespoon of tomato paste,*
- *3 cloves of garlic,*
- *1 cup of water,*
- *salt and pepper.*

Prepare the artichokes by breaking off the outer leaves. When you have peeled down to the tender leaves, trim them a little lower than the original breaking point with scissors. Remove the choke (the hairy center growth).

In a large enamel or cast iron casserole, heat 5 tablespoons of the olive oil and warm gently. Add the minced onions, mushrooms, salt and pepper. Then place the artichokes flat against the bottom of the casserole.

Add the tomato paste, the cup of dry white wine, the cup of water, and the crushed garlic.

Cook on a brisk fire, covering the casserole.

Serve, filling the artichokes with half of the sauce, the other half to be added according to one's taste.

It is very important to prepare the raw vegetables perfectly. None of the artichoke fibers should be found in the dish, since it will be eaten entirely.
The artichoke leaves should not be torn, but broken off with a backward twist.

Barigoulo is provençal term which refers only to the preparation of artichokes.

Artichauts rissolés à l'huile d'olive
Browned hearts artichokes

For six persons :
- *4 pounds of purple baby artichokes,*
- *2 large white onions, minced,*
- *1 large lettuce leaf (Boston),*
- *¼ pound of smoked bacon,*
- *2 cups of olive oil (approximately),*
- *salt and pepper.*

Prepare the artichokes, breaking off the outer leaves. Trim the ends of the leaves with scissors.

Quarter them, remove the choke, if there is any. Usually, in the small purple artichokes the choke is negligible.

In an enamel or cast iron casserole, heat one cup of olive oil until very hot. Add the smoked bacon, sliced very thinly, and the minced onions, with the lettuce leaf cut into large pieces.

As soon as the onions are lightly coloured, add the artichokes, mix well with a wooden spatula. Add salt and pepper and the remaining olive oil.

After 15 minutes on a high flame, scrape the bottom with a spatula to prevent burning, then cover and simmer for about 20 minutes.

This dish is actually another way to prepare Artichokes barigoulo, and I much prefer it that way as the artichokes keep their own flavor and are a great garnish for all grilled meats and poultry.

Aubergines farcies « au maigre »
Stuffed eggplants

For six persons :
- *6 very firm eggplants,*
- *1 large bunch of fresh parsley,*
- *1 large head of garlic,*
- *1 cup of breadcrumbs,*
- *¾ cup of olive oil,*
- *salt and pepper.*

Cut the eggplants in two, lengthwise, without peeling them.

With a teaspoon, scoop out as much flesh as possible. Reserve it.

Place the eggplant shells, flesh side up, in a roasting pan.

Sautée the reserved flesh in a little olive oil with salt and pepper.

Make a stuffing of the finely minced parsley, the chopped garlic, the cooked flesh of the eggplants, the breadcrumbs, and pepper.

Fill the eggplant shells with the mixture. Add a dot of butter on each one. Pour the remaining olive oil generously over them.

Preheat the oven to 450°, then lower to 250° and cook slowly for approximately one hour.

This dish is a perfect garnish for all grilled or roasted meats.

Maigre : without meat or animal fat.

Aubergines frites à la sauce tomate
Fried eggplants with tomato sauce

For six persons : • *6 small eggplants,*
- *2 cups of olive oil (approximately),*
- *3 cups of provençal tomato sauce - (see recipe p. 118),*
- *1 small bunch of parsley,*
- *salt and pepper.*

Wash the eggplants, but do not peel them. Cut them into thin slices, lengthwise.

In a mixing bowl, sprinkle salt over the eggplant slices. This will remove excess water and bitterness. Let stand for about 1 hour. Rinse and pat dry.

Heat the oil in a deep skillet.

Fry the eggplants until golden. Dry them on paper towels to absorb the excess of oil.

Line a serving dish with the fried eggplants, then add a layer of tomato sauce. Repeat the layers until all the eggplants have been used. End with a layer of tomato sauce and sprinkle with the freshly minced parsley.

Eat warm.

Bohémienne
Gypsy

People tend to confuse « Bohémienne » with « Ratatouille ». These two dishes are completely different. Ratatouille comes from Nice, and Bohémienne is a typical « comtadine » recipe.

For six persons :
- *6 eggplants,*
- *6 tomatoes,*
- *1 clove of garlic,*
- *1 cup of olive oil,*
- *4 anchovy fillets, unsalted,*
- *1 tablespoon of flour,*
- *½ glass of milk,*
- *½ cup of breadcrumbs,*
- *salt and pepper.*

Peel and roughly cut the eggplants. Salt them to remove the excess water. Peel, seed, and cut the tomatoes.

In a large saucepan, add ½ cup of olive oil, the eggplants, the tomatoes, the clove of garlic, whole, and the salt and pepper.

As the vegetables are cooking, mash them with a fork, then let them cook slowly.

Into a skillet, pour the rest of the oil and the anchovy fillets. Melt them and add the tablespoon of flour and the milk. Mix well with a wooden spoon to make a sauce.

Add this sauce to the eggplants and tomatoes. Pour this mixtuxe into a baking dish.

Sprinkle with beadcrumbs and heat a few minutes in the oven until the top is golden.

Serve hot.

Comtadine : from the Comtat Venaissin (Avignon) which is the heart of Provence. It once belonged to the popes. Their proprietorship ended in the eighteenth century.

Caviar d'aubergines
Eggplant caviar

For six persons :
- *6 large eggplants,*
- *2 white onions, finely minced,*
- *5 tablespoons of olive oil,*
- *1 small bunch of parsley,*
- *2 tablespoons of wine vinegar,*
- *salt and pepper.*

Wash the eggplants. Do not peel them. Cut them in two, lengthwise.

Preheat the oven to 500°. Roast the eggplants, lowering the heat to 325° (they should not burn).

Remove the pulp and mash it thoroughly ; add the minced onions, salt and pepper.

Incorporate the vinegar and the chopped parsley. Mix well.

Refrigerate and serve very cold.

This caviar may be served as an appetizer on a small serving dish, or spread on grilled French bread with heavy cream.

This dish is also known as poor man's caviar.

Champignons farcis à ma façon
Stuffed mushrooms my way

For four persons :
- *8 large mushrooms (cèpes) or 14 large white mushrooms,*
- *4 shallots,*
- *6 tomatoes, peeled, seeded and cut,*
- *1 slice of cooked ham,*
- *4 anchovies,*
- *8 tablespoons of olive oil,*
- *2 - 3 sage leaves,*
- *parsley and chervil,*
- *salt and pepper.*

Rinse the mushrooms well, cut the stems which should be reserved for later, and remove most of the inside flesh.

In a skillet, sautée the mushrooms slowly in 4 tablespoons of olive oil. Set aside.

In the same skillet, add olive oil, tomatoes, the flesh and the stems of the mushrooms, the chopped shallots, the minced anchovies, the ham cut into very small pieces, the parsley, the chervil and the sage. Salt and pepper.

Fill the inside of the reserved mushrooms with the stuffing.

Reheat for a few minutes in the oven.

Serve hot.

Fresh cèpes, (or boletus) are seldom found in markets outside of Europe. You can use as a substitute large white mushrooms.

Croquettes d'aubergines
Crunchy balls of eggplants

For six persons :
- *4 large eggplants,*
- *½ pound of white chicken meat,*
- *3 slices of white bread,*
- *4 ounces of grated Swiss cheese or Parmesan,*
- *3 eggs,*
- *1 bunch of parsley,*
- *2 cloves of garlic,*
- *6 tablespoons of breadcrumbs,*
- *1 cup of milk,*
- *olive oil, for frying,*
- *salt and pepper.*

Peel the eggplants and slice them, lenghwise. Salt them and let stand ½ hour to remove their excess water.

Dry them.

Heat the oil in a skillet and fry the eggplants a few minutes on each side. When they are cooked, put them aside.

Soak the bread in the milk.

Chop very finely the eggplants, the cooked chicken, the garlic, and the parsley.

Separate the egg whites from the yolks. Place the yolks in a mixing bowl. Beat the egg whites until they form soft peaks.

Drain the bread, squeezing it in your hand, and put it into the mixing bowl with the egg yolks. Add the mixture of eggplants, chicken, parsley, garlic and the grated cheese. Salt and pepper.

Mix all ingredients well until they form a smooth paste.

Form small balls with this paste, then, one at a time, dip them in the beaten egg whites, and roll them delicately in the breadcrumbs.

In a deep skillet, heat the remaining olive oil. When it is very hot, dip the balls into the oil and fry for approximately 5 minutes, turning them from time to time. Remove them with a slotted spoon and drain them on paper towels. Place them on a heated platter, sprinkling with the remaining parsley. Serve with a green salad, dressed with garlic and olive oil.

Courgettes à la provençale
Zucchini provençal

For four persons :
- *2 pounds of zucchini,*
- *1 pound of tomatoes, peeled, seeded, and cut,*
- *½ cup of olive oil,*
- *4 large cloves of garlic,*
- *1 pinch of sugar,*
- *1 pat of butter,*
- *parsley, thyme, and 2 bay leaves,*
- *salt and pepper.*

Wash and dice the zucchini.

In a casserole, heat ¼ cup of the olive oil. When hot, add the zucchini and fry briskly. Salt and pepper.

When golden, place in a colander and let them drain.

In a baking dish, add the remaining olive oil, the pat of butter, and heat slowly on the top of the stove. Place the tomatoes with a pinch of sugar (to reduce the acidity), the thyme, bay leaves, garlic and chopped parsley. Cook for 5 minutes.

Very delicately, mix the zucchini with the tomatoes. Seal the baking dish with aluminum foil and bake in a 350° oven.

Serve very hot.

This side dish is wonderful with all roast or grilled meats.

Gateau de poireaux
Leek cake

For six persons :
- *2 pounds of leeks (white parts only),*
- *¾ pound of smoked bacon,*
- *3 shallots,*
- *3 eggs,*
- *1 sprig of thyme, 1 bay leaf,*
- *2 tablespoons of parsley,*
- *1 ½ cup of milk,*
- *1 large tablespoon grated Swiss or Parmesan cheese,*
- *2 tablespoons of olive oil,*
- *salt and pepper.*

Cut the whites of the leeks into small pieces. Finely chop the smoked bacon.

In a large saucepan, melt the leeks in olive oil, stirring often. When they are soft, add the minced shallots, the 2 tablespoons of parsley, the crushed bay leaf, and the sprig of thyme.

Beat the eggs like for an omelette.

Remove the leeks from the fire and pour the beaten eggs in, with the smoked bacon. Mix well. Add the milk, salt and pepper.

Pour everything into a baking dish. Spinkle with the Swiss cheese.

Bake in hot oven 425°, for 35 minutes, checking the color from time to time.

Serve with roasted meats.

Gratin de courgettes
Zucchini « au gratin »

For six persons :
- *8 zucchini,*
- *3 tomatoes,*
- *2 cloves of garlic, crushed,*
- *1 large white onion,*
- *2 tablespoons of chopped parsley,*
- *1 teaspoon of thyme,*
- *3 tablespoons of grated Swiss or Parmesan cheese,*
- *5 tablespoons of olive oil,*
- *salt and pepper.*

Wash and slice the zucchini.

In a skillet, cook slowly the crushed garlic in olive oil and add the zucchini. Simmer slowly until the water has evaporated.

Drain the cooked zuccini in a colander.

Add some more olive oil to the skillet, plus the chopped onions, the tomatoes (peeled, seeded, and cut), then the thyme and cook for about 20 minutes. Salt and pepper to taste.

Take a baking dish, place half the zucchini in the bottom, pepper well, and add half the grated Swiss cheese and half the tomatoes.

Fill the rest of the dish the same way and finish with the remaining grated cheese.

Bake in hot oven for approximately 15 minutes to obtain a golden crust, but check the color.

Serve hot.

Gratin méridional
Mediterranean gratin

For six persons :
- *1 ½ pounds of tomatoes,*
- *1 ½ pounds of zucchini,*
- *1 ½ pounds eggplants,*
- *3 white onions,*
- *5 tablespoons of grated Swiss or Parmesan cheese,*
- *2 tablespoons of breadcrumbs,*
- *5 tablespoons of olive oil,*
- *salt and pepper.*

Wash, dry, and slice the zucchini. Peel the eggplants and slice them also.

Boil a large quantity of salted water (about 3 quarts) in a pot. Blanch the zucchini and the eggplants for about 5 minutes. Set aside.

Wash, dry and cut the tomatoes into thick slices. Set aside.

Slice the onions and melt them slowly in 3 tablespoons of olive oil until translucent.

Line the bottom of a baking dish with the onions and in succession, cover with one layer of uncooked tomatoes, one layer of zucchini, one layer of eggplants. Between each layer season to taste with salt, pepper, and grated cheese.

Repeat the procedure until you have used all the vegetables. The last layer should be tomatoes.

Cover with breadcrumbs and bake in oven (325°) for about 30-35 minutes.

This delicious gratin is a great garnish for all roasted meats.

Riz camarguais aux courgettes
« Camarguais » rice with zucchini

For six persons :
- *¾ pound of short grain rice,*
- *4 zucchini,*
- *3 ounces of butter,*
- *3 tablespoons of grated Swiss cheese,*
- *1 pinch of grated nutmeg,*
- *salt and pepper.*

Rinse the rice under cold water. Drain. Into a saucepan pour the rice and twice its volume of water. (Approximately 2 cups of rice to 4 cups of water). Bring slowly to a boil.

In the meantime, wash and slice the zucchini. Throw them into the boiling water, reduce heat. Add salt and pepper. Add the pinch of nutmeg. Cover the pan. Simmer for 20 minutes.

When the rice is cooked, stir in the butter and the grated cheese, incorporating them slowly.

Serve with all grilled meats and a good chilled rosé wine.

Camargue : a marshy desertland in southern France - a land of gypsies and rice paddies.

Tarte provençale
Provençal pie

For six persons :
    Pie paste :
- *1 cup of flour,*
- *¼ pound of butter,*
- *4 tablespoons of water,*
- *1 pinch of salt.*

    Filling :
- *3 eggs,*
- *1 cup of "bohémienne" (see Vegetables, p. 35)*
- *1 small container of heavy cream.*

Prepare the paste by mixing the butter and the flour, then add the water and the salt. Let stand for 2 hours.

Preheat the oven at 500°.

Roll out the paste. Butter an 8 inches pie plate. Line with the paste.

Beat together the eggs, the cream, and the « bohémienne », and fill the pie plate.

Bake for 30 minutes.

Serve hot.

Tomates farcies
Stuffed tomatoes

For six persons :
- *12 tomatoes,*
- *¾ pound of sausage meat, or meat leftover,*
- *2 white onions,*
- *6 slices of white bread,*
- *1 cup of milk,*
- *2 eggs,*
- *breadcrumbs,*
- *2 tablespoons of chopped parsley,*
- *salt and pepper.*

Soak the bread slices in milk.

Cut the tops of the tomatoes off, and reserve. Scoop out the pulp, the juice and the seeds. Salt the insides slightly, then turn them over to drain .

Then prepare the following filling : Sautée the minced onions until brown. Add the tomato tops, which have also been finely chopped, the sausage meat (or meat leftover), the drained bread, and 1 tablespoon of chopped parsley. Salt and pepper.

Sautée the filling in olive oil for about 8-10 minutes, remove from the fire and add the eggs - mixing everything thoroughly.

Fill the tomatoes, sprinkle with beadcrumbs and several drops of olive oil.

Place them side by side in a baking dish. Bake in the preheated oven (400º), for approximately 30 minutes.

Serve hct.

Eggs, Omelettes and Custards

« Crespeou »

For eight persons :
- *16 eggs,*
- *3 small artichokes,*
- *2 tomatoes, or 2 tablespoons of tomato sauce,*
- *fresh basil,*
- *2 roasted red peppers,*
- *2 roasted green peppers,*
- *1 eggplant,*
- *thyme and bay leaves,*
- *4 white onions (medium),*
- *2 tablespoons of tapenado (see recipe, p. 121),*
- *chives, parsley and tarragon,*
- *chervil,*
- *1 clove of garlic, crushed,*
- *olive oil for cooking,*
- *salt and pepper.*

You will need about 8 small mixing bowls to keep all of the preparations separate.

Clean the artichokes and keep only the bottoms. Quarter them.

Cook them slowly in hot olive oil with half a minced onion, some thyme, and 1 bay leaf. Salt and pepper. Once they are cooked, approximately 25 minutes, purée them with a fork or a mixer. Set aside in a bowl, add two beaten eggs, and mix well.

Roast the red and green peppers in a hot oven. Peel them and dice them separately very finely.

In a small bowl, add 2 beaten eggs with the red peppers. Salt and pepper. Set aside.

Follow the same procedure for the green peppers - eggs, salt and pepper, set aside.

Dice the eggplant in very small pieces without peeling it. Cook in very hot olive oil with thyme, bay leaf, half a minced onion, and the clove of garlic, crushed.

Salt and pepper. After approximately 25 minutes, purée or mash with a fork. Set aside in a small bowl, with 2 beaten eggs.

Mince the remaining 3 onions, then sautée in hot olive oil until golden. Add thyme, bay leaf, salt and pepper. Purée or mash. Set aside in a small bowl, with 2 beaten eggs.

Beat another 2 eggs in a small bowl. Add the finely chopped tomatoes or the tomato sauce and 2-3 leaves of chopped basil. Salt and pepper, then set aside.

Follow the same procedure for the tapenado and again for the chiselled fresh herbs : tarragon, chives, parsley, and chervil.

Take a small omelette pan, rub it with olive oil.

Make a small omelette with each of the preparations above.

These omelettes should be very flat, very thin, and barely cooked.

In a soufflé dish or in a deep dish, one deep enough to hold the eight omelettes, layer them carefully, one by one. Use your imagination and your sense of color in stacking them, keeping in mind that it will be sliced like a layer cake for serving.

Press them together with a plate to weigh it down. Refrigerate. They will become a compact cake.

Serve cold, cutting it into thin slices and serve, with black olives and cornichons.

This recipe may seem tedious to prepare, but I am sure that you will find the result worthwhile.

Crespeou is the provençal word for small pancakes/small omelettes.

Flan au basilic
Basil custard

For six persons : • *6 fillets of fish, such as whiting, pollack, hake, flounder,*
  • *1 cup of heavy cream,*
  • *1 tablespoon of butter,*
  • *5 eggs,*
  • *4 tablespoons of freshly chiseled basil,*
  • *4 cups of fish stock (see recipe p. 74),*
  • *salt and pepper.*

Simmer the fillets of fish in the fish stock no longer than 3 minutes. Remove with a slotted spoon. Set aside.

Butter a baking dish.

Beat the eggs, the cream, the basil, salt and pepper.

Line the dish with the fillets. Pour the egg mixture over them.

Cook in a bain-marie in a preheated oven (350°) for 35-40 minutes.

Cool and refrigerate.

Unmold only when very cold. To do so, dip the bottom of the dish in very hot water and turn over on a plate, tapping the bottom.

Bain-marie : double saucepan or water bath.

Oeufs aux sardines
Eggs stuffed with sardines

For six persons :
- *6 eggs,*
- *1 can of sardines (packed in olive oil),*
- *1 bunch of parsley,*
- *salt and pepper.*

Place the eggs in salted boiling water. Boil for 10 minutes.

Rinse them under cold water, peel them and cut in two, lengthwise.

Remove the yolks, mash them.

Remove the main bone of the sardines, then chop them roughly.

Chop the parsley.

Make a filling with the mashed egg yolks, the sardines, and the parsley. Salt and pepper.

Fill the egg white shells with the mixture.

Display them on a serving platter garnished with parsley.

Omelette à l'huile d'olive et à la tomate
Omelette with tomatoes and olive oil

For six persons :
- *8 eggs,*
- *2 pounds of tomatoes, peeled or crushed,*
- *1 white onion,*
- *1 clove of garlic,*
- *dry spices : Thyme, rosemary, bay leaf,*
- *fresh basil,*
- *5 tablespoons of olive oil,*
- *salt and pepper.*

In a skillet, sautée 2 tablespoons of olive oil, the minced onion, the tomatoes, the crushed garlic and the dry spices.

Cook on a high fire until all of the water has evaporated. Add salt and pepper.

Then break the eggs in a large mixing bowl, add the cooked tomatoes, and 2 tablespoons of uncooked olive oil. Mix well.

In another pan, heat the remaining olive oil and cook your omelette on a brisk fire.

Serve on a heated platter, sprinkled with the finely chiseled basil.

Omelette aux poivrons
Green pepper omelette

For six persons : • *6 eggs,*
• *2 large green peppers,*
• *1 tablespoon of olive oil,*
• *salt and pepper.*

Wash and cut the green peppers in two, then remove all seeds. Cut into thin ribbons.

Beat the eggs. Salt and pepper.

Heat the olive oil in a skillet, add the green peppers and cook for 10 minutes, stirring from time to time.

Then pour the eggs over the peppers and finish the omelette.

Serve on a heated platter.

« Papeton » d'aubergines
Eggplant custard

For six persons :
- *10 eggplants,*
- *2 cloves of garlic,*
- *3 shallots,*
- *1 cup of heavy cream,*
- *6 tablespoons of olive oil,*
- *4 eggs,*
- *thyme and 2 bay leaves,*
- *tomato sauce (see recipe, p. 118),*
- *nutmeg,*
- *salt and pepper.*

Peel and dice the eggplants.

Heat the olive oil in a casserole, add the eggplants, the garlic, the minced shallots, the thyme and the bay leaves. Salt and pepper.

Cook, uncovered, on low fire for 35 minutes. When the eggplants are cooked, purée trough a food processor or better still, trough a fine mesh sieve to remove the seeds.

Beat the eggs, the puréed eggplants, the cream and the nutmeg. Mix all the ingredients thoroughly.

Pour the mixture into a buttered soufflé dish or a charlotte mold and cook in a bain-marie in a hot oven 450° for 45 minutes.

Cool, refrigerate and unmold.

Serve with a spicy tomato sauce.

Piperade
Delicacy of green and red peppers

For six persons :
- *¾ pound of large red peppers,*
- *¾ pound of green peppers,*
- *1 bunch of parsley,*
- *3 cloves of garlic,*
- *5 tablespoons of olive oil,*
- *salt and pepper.*

Wash the red and green peppers, cut them in two, seed and chop them.

Heat the olive oil in a skillet, add the peppers, the chopped parsley, and the minced garlic. Cover.

Cook slowly for 30 minutes, uncover, add salt and pepper, and continue cooking until all water has evaporated.

Cool. Refrigerate, and serve very cold.

Sea food

Darnes de saumon gratinées
Salmon steak "au gratin"

For six persons :
- *6 salmon steaks,*
- *2 tablespoons of chopped parsley,*
- *2 cups of provençal tomato sauce (see recipe, p. 118),*
- *1 tablespoon of grated Swiss cheese,*
- *1 tablespoon of butter,*
- *salt and pepper.*

Melt the butter in a skillet.

Add the salmon steaks when the butter is foaming. Salt and pepper.

Cook 2-3 minutes on each side, according to size.

Place the steaks in a baking dish, and pour the tomato sauce over them.

Sprinkle with the grated cheese and the parsley.

Bake in a preheated oven (425°) for about 15 minutes or until golden.

Serve hot.

Daurade au four
Sea bass

For six persons :
- *1 sea bass - about 3 ½ - 4 pounds - or black fish,*
- *½ pound of white onions,*
- *3 pounds of potatoes,*
- *4 large ripe tomatoes,*
- *2 cloves of garlic,*
- *4 tablespoons of breadcrumbs,*
- *2 tablespoons of chopped parsley,*
- *1 teaspoon of thyme,*
- *5 tablespoons of olive oil,*
- *salt and pepper.*

Have the fish scaled and cleaned, without removing the head.

Wash and dry the fish, and sprinkle with salt and pepper.

Mince the onions. Peel and mince the potatoes. Mix them with the thyme and the salt and pepper. Rub a baking dish with garlic. Arrange the potatoes and onions in the dish. Pour just enough water to barely cover, then add 4 tablespoons of olive oil.

Preheat oven (350"). The potatoes/onions mixture should bake until there is no water left and it is golden.

In the meantime, cut the tomatoes in two, seed them, salt them, then set aside.

Chop the parsley and the garlic, add the breadcrumbs and mix.

Rinse and drain the tomatoes and fill them with the parsley, garlic, breadcrumb stuffing.

Place the fish on the cooked potatoes. Rub it with the olive oil and arrange the stuffed tomatoes around it. Add a drop of olive oil and a pinch of thyme to each tomato.

Put the baking dish back in the oven and when the fish begins to turn golden, brush it lightly with oil.

When a knife pierces easily through the back of the fish, it is ready.

Encornets farcis
Stuffed squids

For six persons :
- *8 whole squids,*
- *¼ pound of bacon,*
- *½ cup of rice,*
- *10 medium small white onions,*
- *2 cloves of garlic,*
- *3 tablespoons of chopped parsley,*
- *1 teaspoon of thyme leaves,*
- *1 "bouquet garni" (see herbs p. 12),*
- *2 teaspoons of tomato paste,*
- *8 tablespoons of olive oil,*
- *1 cup of dry white wine,*
- *1 egg,*
- *6-12 small toothpicks,*
- *salt and pepper.*

Try to find the squids whole, and, if possible, of the same size. Have them cleaned. Cut off the heads.

Chop the squid heads with 6 white onions, the bacon, the parsley, and two whole squids. Sautée the mixture in olive oil for 5 minutes. Add the rice, which has already been parboiled (blanched) and drained. Salt and pepper.

Fill each squid with this filling and close them with toothpicks.

In a casserole, melt the 4 remaining onions minced in the rest of the olive oil. Toss in the squids and cook until they are golden. Add the white wine, the garlic, the thyme, the "bouquet garni" and the tomato paste. Salt and pepper.

Simmer for 45 minutes.

Make a mayonnaise and gradually add some of the sauce from the squids.

Place the squids on a heated serving platter, and top with the sauce.

Frozen squids are usually fine in the American markets.
To blanch : to plunge food into salted boiling water for a few minutes until it has softened or wilted. Then proceed with your recipe.

Fricassée de petits supions
Stew of baby squids

For six persons :
- *4 pounds of very tender calamari (squids),*
- *4 cloves of garlic,*
- *5 sprigs of parsley,*
- *2 ounces of butter,*
- *5 tablespoons of dry white wine,*
- *$\frac{1}{4}$ cup of heavy cream,*
- *2 pounds of crushed tomatoes,*
- *salt and pepper.*

Clean, wash and dry the baby squids.

Melt the butter in a casserole until it foams, then add the squids and toss rapidly.

When they turn pink (approximately 3 minutes) cut the fire and let them stand in the butter for 5 more minutes. They are cooked at this point. Remove them and set aside on a hot platter.

In the cooking liquid left in the casserole put the tomatoes and white wine. Add the minced parsley and the crushed cloves of garlic. Cook to reduce the sauce while stirring with a wooden spoon to prevent sticking.

Pour in the heavy cream and mix well. Reheat the squids in this sauce on a very low fire for 5 - 10 minutes.

Serve hot on a bed of rice.

Gambas frits au beurre de Montpellier
Fried shrimps with Montpellier butter

For six persons :
- *18 medium sized shrimps,*
- *1 cup of butter Montpellier (See recipe page 123),*
- *4 tablespoons of olive oil,*
- *salt and pepper.*

Heat the olive oil in a skillet.

Fry the shrimps approximately 5 minutes on each side. Add pepper.

When the shrimps are cooked, place them in another skillet, and cover with the Montpellier butter. Simmer on a very low flame, for less than 3 minutes.

Serve very hot.

Gratin de moules aux épinards
Mussels and spinach "au gratin"

For six persons :
- *3 pounds of large mussels,*
- *2 shallots,*
- *1 pound of frozen spinach (whole),*
- *3 tablespoons of olive oil,*
- *3 tablespoons of flour,*
- *1 tablespoon of butter,*
- *2 cups of heavy cream,*
- *3 tablespoons of grated Swiss cheese,*
- *salt and pepper.*

Wash the mussels.

Place them in a large braising pan with the minced shallots. Cover and cook on a high flame for 10 minutes ; the mussels should open by that time.

Shell the mussels and pour the cooking liquid through a fine sieve. Set aside.

Cook the frozen spinach in salted boiling water for about 5 minutes. Then drain it, chop it, and sautée it in olive oil.

In a large skillet, melt the butter, mix in the flour with a wooden spoon, and pour in the reserved liquid from the mussels. Add the heavy cream and pepper. Simmer for 5 minutes.

In a baking dish, mix the mussels, the spinach and the sauce. Spinkle with the grated cheese.

Bake in a preheated oven (425°) for 10 minutes.

I recommend a good chilled Châteauneuf white wine with this dish.

Loup grillé
Grilled bass

For four persons :
- *4 small sea bass, striped bass, snapper, or black fish, approximately ½ pound each,*
- *4 sprigs of fresh tarragon ,*
- *4 twigs of fennel or 1 tablespoon of fennel seeds,*
- *¼ pound of butter,*
- *fresh basil leaves,*
- *salt and pepper.*

Have the fish cleaned but not scaled. Wash them and pat them dry.

Preheat your oven to 500° for about 30 minutes.

Inside each fish, place a sprig of tarragon, a twig of fennel, some fennel seeds, salt and pepper. Also salt and pepper the fish on each side.

Place them in the broiler on aluminum foil and broil each side for 10 minutes.

In the meantime, melt the butter in a skillet with the tarragon and the basil leaves finely chopped.

The butter should remain foamy for serving.

Serve the fish with the butter sauce.

Moules à la tomate
Mussels with tomato sauce

For six persons :
- *4 pounds of mussels,*
- *3 shallots,*
- *1 bunch of parsley,*
- *1 small can of tomato paste,*
- *2 tablespoons of butter for kneaded butter,*
- *1 teaspoon of flour,*
- *pepper.*

Clean the mussels thoroughly.

Place them in a braising pan on a high flame, to open them.

Remove and discard one half of each shell.

Arrange the mussels in a baking dish. Keep warm.

Using the sieved mussel pan liquid, add the small can of tomato paste, the 3 minced shallots, and the chopped parsley.

Blend the butter and the flour into a smooth paste, using a fork.

Add to the mussel liquid, stirring for one minute with a wooden spoon.

Add pepper.

Pour over the mussels.

Serve hot.

Moules au vert
Mussels with green sauce

For six persons :
- *4 pounds of mussels,*
- *2 bunches of parsley,*
- *2 bunches of fresh basil,*
- *1 bunch of chives,*
- *1 large head of garlic,*
- *1 pint of dry white wine,*
- *4 tablespoons of butter,*
- *3 tablespoons of corn meal,*
- *pepper.*

Clean the mussels thoroughly.

Place them in a covered saucepan on a high flame to open them.

As soon as they are opened, remove half the shell of each mussel. Arrange the mussels on a hot platter.

Pour the cooking juice through a sieve and set aside.

Chop finely the parsley, the basil, the chives, and the garlic.

Melt the butter in a skillet, add all of the herbs and garlic, and cook for 2-3 minutes until wilted, stirring all the time with a wooden spoon.

Slowly stir in the corn meal and gradually the wine. The sauce should thicken. Then pour in the reserved juice of the mussels.

Stir again until it coats the spoon. It should stay very smooth. Add pepper.

Pour the sauce over the mussels.

This dish may be eaten hot or cold.

Pain de crabe
Crab custard

For six persons :
- *2 cans of crabs,*
- *2 pounds of monk fish or black fish, bass, halibut, or any other firm fleshed fish,*
- *10 eggs,*
- *2 tablespoons of tomato paste,*
- *1 lemon,*
- *1 fish stock or clam juice (see recipe p. 74),*
- *salt and pepper.*

Parboil the fish in the fish stock for no longer than 3 minutes. Add the juice of one lemon.

Drain and remove the bones.

Flake the fish and the crabs. Mix together.

Beat the eggs with the tomato paste. Add the crab and the fish, then mix thoroughly.

Oil a soufflé dish, pour in the mixture of eggs, fish, and tomatoes. Salt and pepper. Be generous with the pepper. (The fish and crabs may be bland, in which case, I recommend using cayenne).

Prepare a bain-marie and cook in the oven (375°) for one hour.

Let cool. Unmold and refrigerate.

Serve on shredded lettuce and decorate with slices of hardboiled eggs, black olives and quartered tomatoes.

This dish may be prepared a day in advance.

Bain-marie - This cooking method consists in placing a baking dish with food into a larger cooking vessel containing water, maintained at a gentle boil.

Salade pêcheur
Fisherman's salad

For eight persons :

> *Salad :*
> - *6 pounds of mussels,*
> - *2 pounds of small squids,*
> - *2 pounds of shrimps, already cooked,*
> - *6 large potatoes,*
> - *fish stock or clam juice.*
>
> *Sauce :*
> - *2 eggs,*
> - *2 tablespoons of green or red pepper sauce (see recipe, p. 120),*
> - *1 cup of cream,*
> - *1 tablespoon of cognac,*
> - *1 pinch of hot pimento, or cayenne,*
> - *1 cup of olive oil.*

Have the small squids cleaned or buy them frozen, already prepared.

Cook them until they are tender in the fish broth or clam juice. Save the cooking liquid.

Open the mussels by placing them in a saucepan on a hot fire, for about 15 minutes. Save the juice. Remove the shells.

Peel the shrimps.

Combine and mix the squids, the mussels, and the shrimps in a salad bowl.

In the meantime, cook the peeled potatoes in the cooking broth squids. They should not be overcooked, just « al dente ». Dice the potatoes and add to the salad bowl with the seafood.

To prepare the sauce : make a mayonnaise with the eggs and the olive oil, then add the poivron sauce, the pinch of cayenne, the cognac, and the cream. Salt and pepper.

Pour this sauce in the salad bowl. Mix and refrigerate.

Serve very cold with a dry white wine.

Salade de petits supions
Salad of baby squids

For six persons :
- *2 pounds of very tender baby squids,*
- *3 cloves of garlic,*
- *1 bunch of parsley,*
- *1 bunch of chervil, or 1 tablespoon of dry chervil,*
- *fish stock (see recipe, p. 74) or clam juice,*
- *several fennel sprigs,*
- *olive oil,*
- *1 lemon,*
- *salt and pepper.*

In a large saucepan, cook the squids in the fish stock. Bring to a boil, then simmer for 25 minutes.

Drain them, and squeeze the lemon juice over them.

Prepare a vinaigrette dressing in a salad bowl, toss in the squids, the finely chopped parsley, the crushed garlic, and the chiselled fresh chervil.

Add some more olive oil. Salt and pepper.

Serve very cold.

Beignets de sardines
Sardine fritters

For six persons : • *12 fresh sardines, or 12 large fresh smelts,*
• *1 ½ cups of flour,*
• *1 egg,*
• *5 tablespoons of water,*
• *2 cups of olive oil,*
• *salt and pepper.*

Clean the sardines, cut the heads off and remove the bones. Sautée the sardine fillets very lightly in olive oil.

Prepare the fritter batter : mix the flour, the egg yolk, and the water. Salt. Let stand for 30 minutes. Beat the egg white until it forms soft peaks. Stir it delicately into the batter.

Heat the oil in a deep skillet until it smokes. Dip the sardines in the batter, then into the hot oil. Leave in until they are golden.

Remove with a slotted spoon and drain them on paper towels.

Serve hot, with a green salad and garlic croutons.

This recipe was given to me by Bernadette, « cuisinière extraordinaire ». She was a very important and remarkable character in our family.

You can use this batter to make brandade* fritters. Substitute the sardines with a tablespoon of brandade which has been dipped into the batter.

* Brandade : dried codfish purée. This is a very popular method of preparing pounded salt cod in Provence. This dish, like many of the specialties of this region, is flavored with garlic and is prepared by stirring vigorously and constantly with a wooden spoon pounded salt cod on moderate heat, adding olive oil little by little.

Sardines farcies
Stuffed sardines

For six persons :
- *18 fresh sardines or 18 fresh smelts,*
- *¾ pound of cooked ham,*
- *¾ pound of smoked lean bacon,*
- *1 tablespoon of bread crumbs,*
- *½ cup of milk,*
- *1 ¼ bunches of Swiss chard (or spinach),*
- *2 egg yolks,*
- *3 slices of white bread,*
- *1 teaspoon of anchovy paste,*
- *1 tablespoon of grated Swiss or Parmesan cheese ,*
- *olive oil for cooking,*
- *salt and pepper.*

Wash the Swiss chard (or spinach). Keep only the leafy parts. Blanch them in salted boiling water.

Soak the white bread in the lukewarm milk.

Blanch the bacon. Chop the bacon, the cooked ham, the Swiss chard (or spinach). Drain the bread, squeezing it with your hand. Combine and mix the bread with the chopped ingredients. Add the anchovy paste, the grated cheese, the egg yolks, and mix thoroughly. Pepper. Cook this stuffing in a skillet with olive oil for 8-10 minutes, stirring constantly. Let it cool.

Clean the sardines, cut the heads off, and open them. Remove the bones.

In an oiled baking dish, place the fillets of sardines, skin side down. Place a large tablespoon of the filling on each fillet and cover with the other half of the sardine fillet, but the skin side up, this time.

Brush the sardines with oil and sprinkle with breadcrumbs.

Preheat oven to 375° and bake for approximately 25 minutes.

Serve the sardines with steamed potatoes.

Thon à la provençale
Tunafish provençal

For six persons :
- *3 large steaks of fresh tuna,*
- *2 tablespoons of breadcrumbs,*
- *3 cloves of garlic,*
- *1 bunch of parsley,*
- *½ cup of olive oil,*
- *salt and pepper.*

Cut the tuna steaks in two, salt and pepper each side. Place them in an oiled baking dish. Pour in the rest of the olive oil. Sprinkle with the breadcrumbs.

Bake in a preheated oven (400º) for approximately 20 minutes, depending on the thickness of the steaks.

Chop the parsley and the garlic. Sprinkle both on the fish steaks 2-3 minutes before they are done.

Court-bouillon
Fish stock

Fill half of a large saucepan with water. Add :

- *1 onion stuck with 1 clove,*
- *2 chopped carrots,*
- *2 bay leaves,*
- *12-14 peppercorns,*
- *1 tablespoon of vinegar,*
- *5 tablespoons of white wine,*
- *1 pinch of salt,*
- *1 pinch of pepper.*

Simmer for 30 minutes.

This is perfect for all poached fish or shellfish.

Marinade pour poisson
Fish marinade

For approximately 2 pounds of fish :
- *1 quart of dry white wine,*
- *1 cup of olive oil,*
- *2 lemons,*
- *4 sprigs of parsley,*
- *2 sprigs of fennel,*
- *12-14 black peppercorns.*

In a mixing bowl, pour the white wine, the olive oil, the 2 lemons (quartered), the parsley, the fennel, and the roughly crushed peppercorns.

Mix with a wisk.

Add the raw fish.

Meat and Poultry

Agneau des Alpilles braisé au thym
Lamb from the Alpilles braised with thyme

For six persons :
- *3 generous pounds of lamb (ask your butcher for the best braising parts : shoulder flat ribs, neck or a mixture of all),*
- *2 large pinches of thyme leaves,*
- *5 white onions,*
- *2 cloves of garlic,*
- *2 tablespoons of olive oil,*
- *2 tablespoons of water,*
- *salt and pepper.*

Usually the meat of lamb and mutton contains enough fat to become golden brown without the assistance of other ingredients.

On low fire, place the pieces of lamb in a large sautée pan until they reach a lovely color. Then, one at a time, place the pieces of meat in a cocotte* where they will cook without oil.

Sprinkle the meat with thyme, salt and pepper.

Add the finely minced onions and the garlic.

Pour in 2 tablespoons of water and 2 tablespoons of olive oil.

Cover the cocotte, then cook on low fire.

From time to time, take off the lid and scrape the juices from the bottom of the pan.

Serve hot, garnished with grilled tomatoes.

* Cocotte : enamel or cast iron casserole with a lid.

Côtes d'agneau à l'olive
Lamb chops with olives

For six persons :
- *12 fairly thick lamb chops,*
- *1 shallot,*
- *5 tablespoons of milk,*
- *2 tablespoons of flour,*
- *¼ pound of black olives, cured in oil,*
- *1 tablespoon of grated Swiss or Parmesan cheese ,*
- *1 tablespoon of butter,*
- *5 tablespoons of olive oil,*
- *1 pinch of grated nutmeg,*
- *½ cup of dry white wine,*
- *salt and pepper.*

In a casserole, heat 4 tablespoons of olive oil, then add the finely minced shallot. Stir in slowly the flour, then the milk ; use a wooden spoon. Add salt and pepper, and the nutmeg. Set aside.

Remove the olive pits. Then chop the olives. Make a tapenado (see recipe, p. 121), adding 2 tablespoons of white wine.

Salt and pepper the lamb chops on each side, and sautée in a skillet with a pat of butter and the olive oil. Do not overcook (3 minutes). Set aside.

Place the lamb chops in a baking dish, and spread them with one layer of olive purée, one layer of the white sauce (béchamel), a sprinkle of grated cheese and a pat of butter.

Bake in a preheated oven (475°) for 5 minutes.

Serve with a green salad with olive oil dressing, and a robust red country wine.

Gigot d'agneau à la crème d'ail
Leg of lamb with cream of garlic

For six persons : • *1 leg of lamb, approximately 3-3 ½ pounds,*
• *6 heads of garlic,*
• *salt and pepper.*

Peel the garlic and put the cloves in a saucepan with cold water. Bring to a boil. Change the water after 10 minutes.

Repeat 4-5 times, making sure the last vat of boiling water is slightly salted.

Then mash the cooked garlic and set aside.

Spit roast your leg of lamb for approximately one hour (10 minutes less if you like it very pink).

When you cut the leg, set aside the juice, and add it gradually to the purée of garlic.

Serve on a heated platter.

The gourmet will discover the difference between the leg of lamb roasted on a spit or in an oven.

Boulettes de viandes à la sauce tomate
Meatballs with tomato sauce

For six persons :
- *1 ½ pounds of ground beef,*
- *¼ pound of ground veal,*
- *¼ pound of ground pork (lean),*
- *2 eggs ,*
- *3 medium white onions,*
- *5 slices of white bread,*
- *1 cup of milk,*
- *1 bunch of parsley,*
- *1 bunch of fresh mint,*
- *1 bay leaf,*
- *1 tablespoon of thyme,*
- *tomato sauce (see sauce recipe, p. 118),*
- *1 cup and 3 tablespoons of breadcrumbs,*
- *1 cup of olive oil,*
- *salt and pepper.*

Soak the bread slices in lukewarm milk for about 30 minutes.

Chop the parsley, the mint, and crumble the bay leaf. Mince the onions. Pepper generously.

In a large mixing bowl, add all the ground meat, the eggs, and the bread, drained and squeezed. Add the herb/onion mixture and mix thoroughly with your hands.

Take a small quantity of this mixture in the palm of your hand and roll to form a small ball, as compact as possible. Proceed the same way with the rest of the mixture.

Take a large skillet and heat the olive oil.

Roll the meatballs in breadcrumbs and fry in hot olive oil for 6-8 minutes. Remove with a slotted spoon when they are golden, and place them on a heated serving platter. Reheat tomato sauce. Pour over the meatballs. Serve on a bed of natural rice.

Daube provençale
Provençal beef stew

For six persons :
- *3-4 pounds of braising meat (top beef round is the best, but you may use chuck pot roast, sirloin top, or bottom round),*
- *¼ pound of smoked bacon, diced,*
- *4 medium onions,*
- *2 carrots,*
- *5 cloves of garlic,*
- *1 clove,*
- *¼ cup of olive oil,*
- *2 bay leaves,*
- *1 teaspoon each of thyme and rosemary,*
- *1 tablespoon of tomato purée,*
- *1 quart of fine red wine, such as Châteauneuf-du-Pape,*
- *salt and 12-14 peppercorns.*

Into a casserole, pour ½ cup of olive oil and the diced bacon. Add the sliced carrots, the quartered onions, the clove, the tomato purée, the cloves of garlic, and the herbs.

Sprinkle with the peppercorns and salt.

Mix the meat, which has been cut into cubes, (approx. 2 inches square), with the vegetables and herbs. Then pour in the red wine.

Cover and let cook on a high flame until it boils. Then lower the fire and simmer for 5 hours.

My success with this traditional provençal dish relies on an even and slow heat throughout the braising.

Serve on a heated platter on a bed of « al dente » macaroni, which has been doused in the sauce.

This stew is even more tasty when reheated the next day.

Brochettes de bœuf au beurre d'herbes
Skewered beef with a herb butter sauce

For six persons :
- *2 pounds of fillet of beef,*
- *3 tablespoons of butter,*
- *2 tablespoons of Dijon mustard, or Maille or any kind of medium hot mustard,*
- *2 tablespoons of dry tarragon, or 4 sprigs of fresh tarragon,*
- *2 tablespoons of chopped parsley,*
- *2 tablespoons of chopped chives,*
- *salt and pepper.*

Ask your butcher to dice the fillet into even pieces, 2-3 inches square.

Build a very hot fire on a barbecue.

Skewer the pieces of meat on the necessary number of skewers.

Roast them on the fire for 10 minutes, turning them from time to time.

Melt the butter in a bain-marie. Salt and pepper. Stir in the mustard, the parsley, the tarragon and the chives (finely chopped).

Mix all of the ingredients well before the butter is totally melted. Be careful not to cook the butter.

When the skewered beef is cooked, arrange it on a heated platter. Salt and pepper.

Serve the sauce in a sauceboat. The sauce shoud be ladled on at once, since it will not hold up for a long time.

Estouffade de bœuf
Smothered beef provençal

For six persons :
- *3 pounds of beef, rump roast flank, round or sirloin tip,*
- *1 pound of small white onions,*
- *1 tablespoon of mustard, Dijon or Maille,*
- *1 small can of anchovy fillets,*
- *1 bay leaf, crumbled,*
- *1 teaspoon of thyme leaves,*
- *1 lemon,*
- *8 tablespoons of olive oil,*
- *salt and pepper.*

Have your butcher (or you) cut the beef in thin slices, about ¼ inch thick.

Mince the onions.

In a casserole or braising dish, heat 6 tablespoons of olive oil. Layer the beef slices on the bottom, then the onions, and repeat the layering with the beef slices and the onions. Salt and pepper, and add the herbs. Cover. Simmer on a very low fire.

When the top layer of onions is melted and the juices are rising to the surface, it is cooked.

Pound the anchovy fillets, whith the mustard until it forms a smooth paste. Add 2 tablespoons of olive oil as you would for a mayonnaise.

Then add the juice of the lemon and pour the sauce over the beef in the cocotte. Heat for 2 minutes.

Serve on a bed of rice.

Pot-au-feu provençal
Provençal pot-au-feu

This dish must be simmered or the meat will become tough and dry.

For six persons :
- *3-4 pounds of stewing beef (top butt, or round, or rump pot roast),*
- *1 bone with the marrow,*
- *3 white turnips,*
- *6 carrots,*
- *6 small leeks,*
- *1 tomato,*
- *1 celery stalk with the leaves,*
- *1 onion stuck with 2 cloves,*
- *2 cloves of garlic,*
- *1 bay leaf,*
- *2 sprigs of fresh thyme, or 1 teaspoon of dry thyme,*
- *4-5 sprigs of parsley,*
- *3 tablespoons of coarse salt,*
- *4-5 black peppercorns,*
- *5 quarts of cold water.*

Pour the cold water into a large soup kettle. Add the meat and the bone with marrow. Salt. Start the heat slowly until it boils. The meat should not be plunged into hot water, or it would become fibrous.

Cover and simmer for approximately 3 ½ hours.

In the meantime, peel and wash the vegetables. Quarter the turnips. Cut the carrots lengthwise. Quarter the tomato. Slice the celery. Cut the leeks in four, lengthwise. After two hours of cooking, add all these vegetables and the onion to the soup kettle.

Remove the rising grease and gristle with a spoon. Add the spices tied in a cheese cloth. When you are ready to serve, remove the bone and keep the marrow. Arrange the meat and the vegetables on a heated platter. Pour the broth into a soup terrine. You may then serve this delicious broth over slices of grilled French bread, spread with the marrow. The meat and vegetables should be served with a good tomato sauce. (See recipe p. 118.)

Canard aux olives
Duck with olives

For six persons :
- *1 duck, about 4 pounds,*
- *½ pound of green olives,*
- *2 tablespoons of olive oil,*
- *1 cup of dry white wine,*
- *2 tomatoes,*
- *1 white onion,*
- *3 cloves of garlic,*
- *1 teaspoon of thyme,*
- *2 bay leaves,*
- *1 small bunch of parsley,*
- *1 teaspoon of flour,*
- *salt and pepper.*

Blanch the olives for about 10 minutes. Mince the onions.

Peel, seed and quarter the tomatoes.

Cut the duck into 6 pieces : breasts, legs, and back. Sautée them in a skillet with the hot olive oil.

Add the tomatoes and the onion. Cook until golden. Sprinkle with flour, salt and pepper.

Pour in the wine. Add the thyme, the bay leaves, the garlic, the drained olives, and a glass of water.

Cover and simmer for one hour. Sprinkle with the chopped parsley.

Serve hot on a bed of white rice, or potatoes.

The best olives for this recipe is the green variety already craked, which are called Naphtliou.

Canard à l'étouffée
Smothered duckling

For six persons :
- *2 small ducks, 3-4 pounds each,*
- *2 pounds of fresh tomatoes,*
- *10 cloves of garlic, crushed,*
- *3 white onions, minced,*
- *¼ pound of green olives*,*
- *10 tablespoons of olive oil,*
- *1 teaspoon of thyme,*
- *salt and pepper.*

Quarter the ducks. Sautée them in a skillet with olive oil until golden, then set aside and discard the oil.

Peel and seed the tomatoes, then cut them. Add the remaining oil to the skillet with the minced onions, the crushed garlic and the tomatoes.

Cook the vegetables on a high fire for 5 minutes. Add the duck pieces, the olives, the thyme, salt and pepper. Cover and cook for another 25 minutes.

Serve on a bed of fresh buttered pasta.

* For this recipe, choose the same kind of olives as for « Duck with olives ».

Dinde farcie
Stuffed Turkey

Stuffed turkey is the traditional provençal Christmas luncheon.

For six persons :
- *1 small turkey (6-8 pounds),*
- *2 pounds of chestnuts (whole canned chestnuts are the best choice),*
- *2 tablespoons of cognac,*
- *6 slices of bacon,*
- *1 pound of sausage meat for stuffing,*
- *5 tablespoons of olive oil,*
- *salt and pepper.*

The day before, marinate the liver of the turkey in the cognac.

Clean the turkey. Season the cavity with salt and pepper. Chop the liver. Mix the sausage meat, with half of the chestnuts and the liver.

Fill the turkey with this stuffing. Sew or skewer the vents. Cover the breast with the bacon slices. Truss the bird.

Preheat the oven to 450°.

Rub the turkey with olive oil.

Place the turkey in a shallow baking dish.

Braise for about 2 hours, basting frequently.

Remove most of the fat from the juices. Pour the sauce into a sauceboat.

Serve the turkey on a platter with the rest of the chestnuts, which have been heated in a bain-marie.

Lapin à l'ail
Rabbit with garlic

For six persons :
- *2 young rabbits,*
- *20 cloves of garlic,*
- *2 tablespoons of olive oil,*
- *10 tablespoons of dry white wine,*
- *¼ cup of brandy,*
- *1 small bunch of parsley,*
- *salt and pepper.*

Have the butcher cut the rabbits.

Heat the oil in a skillet, and brown the pieces of rabbit. Salt and pepper.

When golden, pour in the brandy, ignite and flame.

Add the garlic cloves, peeled, and the white wine.

Bring to a boil, cover and braise for 25 minutes.

Chop the parsley.

Pour the juices into a sauceboat.

Serve on a heated platter.

Sprinkle with the chopped parsley.

You can find frozen rabbit in many supermarkets. It is already cut and should be defrosted the day before.

Lapin à l'anchoïade
Rabbit with anchovy sauce

For six persons :
- *1 rabbit, 3-4 pounds,*
- *18 fillets of anchovies, unsalted, or ¼ pound of anchovy paste,*
- *½ pound of smoked bacon,*
- *20 small white onions,*
- *6 small tomatoes,*
- *5 tablespoons of dry white wine,*
- *pepper.*

Ask the butcher to bone the rabbit, but not to cut it.

Coarsely chop and mash the anchovies. Spread half of the wash of the inside and the outside of the rabbit. Pepper.

Roll and tie the rabbit with strings as to form a roulade (a rolled piece of meat).

Let stand for one hour.

Dice finely the smoked bacon. Sautée the pieces in a skillet until golden. Remove them with a slotted spoon and keep the fat which is in the skillet.

Sautée the rolled rabbit slowly in the bacon rendering until brown.

Add the minced onions, the dry white wine and the diced bacon.

Cover and simmer for about 45 minutes.

In the meantime, peel, seed and halve the tomatoes.

Place them around the rabbit with the remaining mashed anchovies.

Cover and continue the cooking for 30 minutes.

Serve the rabbit cut into slices, with the anchovies and the tomatoes on a bed of white rice.

Epaule de mouton aux flageolets
Lamb shoulder with small lima beans

For six persons :
- *1 lamb shoulder, approximately 3 pounds,*
- *4 slices of white bread,*
- *1 cup of milk,*
- *3 cloves of garlic,*
- *1 cup of mixed fresh tarragon, chives, parsley, and chervil,*
- *1 tablespoon of thyme,*
- *1 egg yolk,*
- *4 tablespoons olive oil,*
- *2 pounds of lima beans,*
- *salt and pepper.*

Ask your butcher to bone the lamb shoulder.

Prepare a stuffing : soak the bread in milk. Crush the garlic. Chisel the fresh herbs.

In a mixing bowl, stir the bread drained and squeezed, the herbs, the garlic, the thyme and the egg yolk. Salt and pepper to taste.

Lightly sautée the stuffing in a skillet with one tablespoon of olive oil.

Spread the boned shoulder on the table.

Fill it with the stuffing, roll the meat and tie it with strings.

Heat 3 tablespoons of olive oil in the casserole. Add the meat and cook on a high flame uncovered, turning it from time to time, for 40 minutes.

Cook the lima beans in boiling salted water. Surround the cooking lamb shoulder with them.

Serve hot.

The sauce can be thinned with the cooking liquid of the lima beans.

Flageolets are rarely found in the United States, but very small lima beans make a statisfactory substitute.

Navarin de mouton
Lamb stew

For six persons :
- *2 ½ pounds of lamb ribs,*
- *3 white onions, minced,*
- *1 tablespoon of flour,*
- *1 pound of carrots,*
- *1 pound of white turnips,*
- *1 teaspoon of thyme,*
- *2 bay leaves,*
- *4 tablespoons of olive oil,*
- *1 glass of water,*
- *salt and pepper.*

Ask your butcher to prepare the lamb ribs.

Heat the oil in a casserole, brown the meat and the minced onions, until golden.

Sprinkle the flour over the meat, add the water, salt and pepper and stir with a wooden spoon.

Slice the carrots, cut the turnips in half, lenghtwise. Add them to the casserole with the thyme and the bay leaves.

Cover and simmer for 1 ½ hours.

Serve hot.

The name of navarin is used expressely for lamb or mutton stew, usually cooked with spring vegetables.

Sauté de mouton aux aubergines
Sautéed lamb with eggplants

For six persons :
- *3 pounds of lamb shoulder,*
- *4 medium eggplants,*
- *2 tomatoes,*
- *1 sprig of thyme,*
- *1 bay leaf,*
- *4 tablespoons of olive oil,*
- *1 glass of water,*
- *salt and pepper.*

Ask your butcher to cut the lamb shoulder into large chunks.

In a casserole, enamel or cast iron, heat the olive oil. Sautée the meat until golden brown. Salt and pepper.

Add the thyme, the bay leaf, crumbled, then the glass of water. Cover and simmer on a low fire.

In the meantime, wash the eggplants, cut them into cubes without peeling them, then salt them to remove excess water. Let stand for ½ hour, then dry them.

Peel, seed and quarter the tomatoes.

Add the vegetables to the meat, and more salt and pepper.

Cook, covered for 25 minutes, then uncovered for 25 minutes more.

Serve on a heated platter, the eggplants in the center, surrounded by the meat.

Filet mignon de porc aux oignons
Pork fillet (loin) with onions

For six persons :
- *1 pork loin, about 2-3 pounds, cleaned and trimmed,*
- *1 pound of large white onions,*
- *4 shallots,*
- *2 sprigs of thyme,*
- *2 bay leaves,*
- *6 tablespoons of olive oil,*
- *salt and pepper.*

Mince the onions and the shallots.

In a cast iron casserole, heat the olive oil. Fry the onions and the shallots. Add the thyme and crumbled bay leaves.

Let the onions and shallots acquire a nice red colour, stirring them occasionally.

With a sharp knife, make a criss-cross pattern on the fillet. Place it in the casserole. Sprinkle generously with salt and pepper.

Cover the casserole. Cook on high fire for 15 minutes on each side, turning it from time to time, until the meat becomes an even golden brown.

Lower the fire and cook, still with the lid on, for 25 minutes. Turn the fillet from time to time.

My secret for this recipe : to prevent the onions and shallots from burning, take them from the bottom of the casserole when you lower the fire (after 15 minutes) and put them on top of the meat. They will add to the smoothness of the sauce.

Petites brochettes de poulet aux herbes
Chicken with herbs on small skewers

For six persons :
- *1 large roasting chicken, 3-4 pounds,*
- *½ quart of olive oil,*
- *2 lemons,*
- *2 sprigs of thyme,*
- *1 sprig rosemary,*
- *2 bay leaves,*
- *2 cloves,*
- *5 juniper berries,*
- *salt and pepper.*

This dish should be prepared the day before.

In a large mixing bowl, pour in the olive oil, the juice of the 2 lemons, the thyme, rosemary, bay leaves, the cloves, and the juniper berries.

Remove the skin from the chicken and as much fat as possible, or even better, ask your butcher to do it.

Cut the white meat of the chicken into small pieces about 1 ½ inches, and put them into the marinade. Let stand for 24 hours.

The next day, place the pieces of chicken on the skewers.

Preheat the oven to 500° or start a barbecue.

Place the skewers on a very hot baking sheet or on the grill of the barbecue. Add salt, pepper and thyme.

They must be well grilled and crackling.

The perfect side dish with them is white rice, sautéed in olive oil. It is delicious.

For the skewers : You can use long wooden sticks. They are available in most supermarkets and/or Oriental stores. You will need 4 sticks per person.

Poulet farci à l'ail
Chicken stuffed with garlic

For six persons :
- *1 roasting chicken of about 3 pounds,*
- *1 head of garlic,*
- *olive oil,*
- *1 small loaf of French or Italian bread,*
- *1 small bunch of thyme,*
- *2 tablespoons of flour,*
- *salt and pepper.*

Cut the bread into small cubes, and brown them in olive oil.

Remove them with a slotted spoon and drain them on paper towels. When cool, rub them with garlic cloves.

Stuff the chicken with the croutons, salt and pepper.

Place it in a cast iron or enamel casserole with the thyme, the rest of the olive oil and the remaining cloves of garlic, unpeeled.

Seal the cover of the casserole by using a ribbon of paste made of flour and water. The lid will be tight that way.

Preheat the oven to 450°, and cook for 2 hours.

Remove the lid and you will find a wonderfully moist and golden chicken, with a delicate flavor.

Poulet en ratatouille
Chicken with ratatouille

For six persons :
- *1 frying chicken, approximately 3 pounds,*
- *6 tomatoes,*
- *5 zucchini,*
- *5 small eggplants,*
- *3 white onions,*
- *2 red or green peppers,*
- *4 cloves of garlic,*
- *thyme,*
- *2 bay leaves,*
- *rosemary,*
- *5 tablespoons of olive oil,*
- *salt and pepper.*

Heat the olive oil in a large casserole. Sautée the pieces of chicken until golden brown. Salt and pepper.

Cut the peppers in two, remove the seeds, and slice thinly.

Wash the zucchini and the eggplants. Do not peel them, but remove the ends.

Cube the eggplants and slice the zucchini. Peel and mince the onions and crush the cloves of garlic. When the pieces of chicken are golden brown, add the vegetables, the onions and the garlic.

Peel the tomatoes by rapidly plunging them into boiling water and rinsing them in cold water. Seed them and coarsely chop them.

When the vegetables are translucent, add the tomatoes, the thyme, the crumbled bay leaves and the rosemary. Add 3 tablespoons of olive oil and correct seasoning if necessary.

Cover and simmer for 15 minutes. Then uncover and cook for 15 minutes more. The ratatouille should be reduced by half.

Arrange the pieces of chicken on a heated serving platter, surrounded by the ratatouille. (Of course, you may also serve the ratatouille on a separate dish).

Côtelettes de veau au basilic
Veal cutlets with basil

For six persons :
- *6 veal cutlets,*
- *½ cup of olive oil,*
- *¼ pound of butter,*
- *3 tablespoons of fresh basil or 3 tablespoons of dry basil,*
- *salt and pepper.*

Brown the cutlets in a hot dry skillet until cooked. Set them aside and keep them warm. Salt and pepper.

In the meantime, mince the fresh basil. Incorporate the oil and butter to form a smooth paste. Add the basil.

Arrange the cutlets on a hot serving platter. Top each of them with a tablespoon of the cream of basil.

Escalopes de veau à la provençale
Veal scallopini provençal

For six persons :
- *6 thin veal scallopini,*
- *6 shallots,*
- *1 clove of garlic,*
- *3 medium tomatoes,*
- *2 tablespoons of olive oil,*
- *salt and pepper.*

Heat the olive oil in a skillet and sautée the scallopini until golden.

Mince the shallots and the garlic. Add them to the scallopini until translucent.

Wash and cut the tomatoes in two. Place them around the veal, add a little olive oil. Salt and pepper.

Cook for 10 more minutes.

Serve very hot.

Poitrine de veau farcie
Stuffed veal breast

For six persons :
- *1 breast of veal, approximately 4 pounds,*
- *1 pound of lean, ground veal,*
- *2 tablespoons of freshly chopped parsley,*
- *1 crushed clove of garlic,*
- *1 large pinch of marjoram,*
- *1 egg,*
- *1 pound of spinach, or if available, Swiss chard,*
- *1 white onion, finely minced,*
- *1 cup of black olives, pitted and chopped,*
- *salt and pepper.*

Prepare a stuffing : steam and drain the spinach or the Swiss chard. Chop them coarsely. Mix in the ground veal, the minced onions, the crushed garlic, the black olives, the marjoram, and the raw egg. Salt and pepper.

Stuff this mixture into the breast of veal. Sew it. Place in a shallow baking pan.

Preheat oven to 425°, and roast for 2 hours. The meat should not be pink.

When it is cooked, cut the breast into slices (about 1 inch).

This is an excellent dish served cold with a green salad.

Foie de veau à la provençale
Calf liver provençal

For six persons :
- *6 thin slices of calf liver,*
- *4 cloves of garlic,*
- *1 small bunch of parsley,*
- *3 tablespoons of butter,*
- *2 large tablespoons of flour,*
- *salt and pepper.*

Dip the slices of liver in the flour, covering them totally. Set them aside on a platter, so that they are not touching each other.

Mince very finely the parsley and the garlic, and mix them.

Melt the butter in the skillet, until it foams, (do not overcook).

Place the slices of liver in the skillet, sprinkle them with the parsley and garlic, salt and pepper. Cook for one minute, then turn them over and repeat the layer of parsley and garlic.

Serve them on a heated platter, pouring the cooking juices over them.

Marinade pour viande blanche
Marinade for white meat

For roughly 2 pounds of meat :
- *1 quart of dry white wine,*
- *5 tablespoons of olive oil ,*
- *1 carrot,*
- *1 onion,*
- *1 bunch of celery,*
- *1 bay leaf, crushed,*
- *1 sprig of thyme,*
- *1 sprig of rosemary,*
- *1 clove of garlic,*
- *3 stems of parsley,*
- *a handful of whole black peppercorns,*
- *2 cloves.*

Peel the carrot and slice it very thinly. Peel the onion and mince it. Chop coarsely the celery. Peel and chop the garlic.

Pour the wine and the olive oil into a large mixing bowl. Add the carrot, the onion, the celery, the garlic, and all of the herbs and spices.

Mix well and marinate the meat for at least 12 hours.

Marinade pour viande rouge
Marinade for red meat

For roughly 2 pounds of meat :
- *1 quart of white wine,*
- *1 carrot,*
- *1 onion,*
- *1 bunch of celery,*
- *2 cloves,*
- *1 clove of garlic,*
- *1 bay leaf,*
- *a handful of black peppercorns.*

Peel the carrot and slice it thinly. Peel the onion and mince it. Crush the garlic. Chop the celery.

Into a large mixing bowl, pour the wine, add the vegetables and the spices.

Mix well and marinate the meat for at least 12 hours.

Patés and Terrines

Caillette aux épinards
Small paté with spinach

For six persons :
- ½ *pound of ground pork,*
- ½ *pound of ground veal,*
- ¾ *pound of spinach, blanched,*
- *1 egg,*
- *3 juniper berries, crushed,*
- *salt and pepper.*

Chop the spinach. Mix all of the ingredients thoroughly and place them in a buttered baking dish.

Place in a bain-marie.

Preheat the oven to 325° and cook approximately one hour in a bain-marie.

Serve hot or cool, (refrigerate). Unmold on a serving platter.

Slice and serve with a chicory salad with garlic and olive oil dressing.

Caillette is the provençal name for paté mixed with herbs and green leafy vegetables, mostly spinach or Swiss chard.

Caillettes provençales aux herbes
Small provençal patés with herbs

For 12 caillettes :
- *2 pounds of pork liver,*
- *½ pound of pork loin,*
- *1 pound of pig's back fat,*
- *2 pork cauls,*
- *6 cloves of galic,*
- *1 pound of spinach,*
- *2 cups of chopped fresh parsley,*
- *2 tablespoons of thyme leaves,*
- *3 bay leaves,*
- *salt and pepper*

Cube all of the meat into pieces of approximately ½ inch square.

Crush the cloves of garlic. Mix with the parsley, the thyme, and the crumbled bay leaves.

Blanch the spinach, fresh or frozen, in salted water, drain it, then chop very finely. Add to the meat and spices.

Arrange the mixture in a terrine, and refrigerate for at least 4 hours.

Wash the cauls in lukewarm water, then spread them onto a wooden board, carefully, as they are very delicate. Cut them into 6 inch squares. Layer the stuffing mixture, (1 ½ large tablespoons on each piece of caul) and then fold them. Form each of them into a ball, and place them in a baking dish.

Preheat the oven to 450°, and cook for one hour, lower the heat to 325°, and cook for an additional 30 minutes.

These caillettes are good hot or cold, and in both cases, should be served with a chicory salad with garlic croutons.

Paper thin slices of salt pork may be substituted for the caul. If using the salt pork, cut 4" by 6" slices and place them as a cross, filling the center with the stuffing. Proceed with them as with the caul.

Terrine aux champignons
Mushroom terrine

For six persons :
- *1 ¼ pounds of white mushrooms,*
- *¾ pound of eggplants,*
- *10 eggs,*
- *1 clove of garlic, crushed,*
- *juice from half a lemon,*
- *1 cup of heavy cream,*
- *5 tablespoons of olive oil,*
- *1 pinch of thyme, rosemary, bay leaves, savory, all crumbled,*
- *salt and pepper.*

Peel the eggplants and dice them. Put through a food processor or a food mill.

Add the eggs, the spices, the lemon juice, the crushed garlic, the salt and pepper.

Clean the mushrooms and chop them coarsely. Place them in a hot dry skillet without any fat. All of the excess water should evaporate.

When they are dry, add a tablespoon of olive oil and sautée them until golden. Drain and set aside.

Whip the heavy cream. Mix with the raw eggplant purée.

Butter a deep baking dish or terrine. Then layer by layer, arrange the mushrooms, the eggplant purée, until the vegetables are all used.

Preheat the oven to 375°. Cook the terrine in a bain-marie for 35 minutes. Let cool for at least 1 hour before serving, or refrigerate for 4-6 hours. Unmold and serve in thin slices.

Terrine de lapin
Rabbit terrine

For six to eight persons :
- *2 young rabbits (or 5 pounds of frozen rabbit),*
- *1 pound of sausage meat,*
- *1 ¼ pound of chicken livers,*
- *5 tablespoons of old port,*
- *1 egg,*
- *1 pork caul,*
- *2 onions,*
- *1 small bunch of parsley,*
- *1 bay leaf,*
- *1 sprig of thyme,*
- *¼ cup of brandy,*
- *12 slices of bacon,*
- *salt and pepper.*

Marinate the chicken livers in the port for 20 minutes. On the day before, have the rabbit boned and cut in small pieces, or defrost it.

In a large mixing bowl, combine the pieces of rabbit with the sausage meat, the egg, the thyme, the chopped parsley, the minced onions. Add the brandy, the salt and pepper.

Line the bottom and side of a terrine or a deep baking dish with the bacon slices. Fill it with half of the paté mixture. Make a layer with the chicken livers, and top with the rest of the mixture. Cover with the remaining bacon slices. Decorate with bay leaves.

Preheat the oven to 350° and cook in a bain-marie for 2 hours.

Cool and refrigerate.

Serve with a cold rosé wine such as Tavel.

Terrine de légumes au four
Baked vegetable terrine

For six persons :
- *¾ pound of tomatoes,*
- *3 green peppers,*
- *3 red peppers,*
- *¼ pound of cooked ham,*
- *½ cup of heavy cream,*
- *5 eggs,*
- *¼ pound of black olives, pitted and chopped,*
- *1 tablespoon of grated Swiss or Parmesan cheese,*
- *1 pinch of thyme,*
- *2 bay leaves,*
- *1 sprig of rosemary,*
- *1 small bunch of parsley,*
- *olive oil,*
- *salt and pepper.*

Peel and seed the tomatoes, then chop them coarsely. Sautée them in a skillet with hot olive oil.

Wash the peppers, slice them in two, lengthwise, seed them, and slice into narrow ribbons. Add them to the cooking tomatoes, the diced ham and the bay leaves, crumbled.

Cook until the vegetables become a smooth paste. Set aside and cool.

Stir in the thyme, the rosemary, the chopped parsley, and the black olives.

In the meantime, beat the eggs with the heavy cream and the grated Swiss cheese.

Mix the vegetable paste and the beaten egg mixture. Pour into a deep baking dish or terrine and cook in a preheated oven in a bain-marie, for 45 minutes.

Check for cooking with a sharp knife blade. It should not run and the terrine should be very compact. Cool, refrigerate and unmold.

Serve cold with a green salad with garlic dressing.

Terrine de lotte à la menthe
Monkfish terrine with fresh mint

For 6 persons :
- *3 pounds of thickly sliced monkfish,*
- *6 sprigs of fresh mint,*
- *1 lemon, very thinly sliced,*
- *1 cup of heavy cream,*
- *6 eggs,*
- *1 "bouquet garni",*
- *3 quarts of fish stock (see recipe, p. 74),*
- *salt and pepper.*

Bring the 3 quarts of fish stock to a boil. Add the mint stems, saving the leaves.

Lower the fire and simmer the fish slices for about 5 minutes. Remove the fish and drain. Let cool.

Flake the fish. Salt and pepper.

Beat the 6 eggs as in an omelette and stir in the flaked fish.

Butter a deep baking dish, line the bottom with some lemon slices and some mint leaves. Fill the dish with the fish and egg mixture. Garnish with fresh mint leaves.

Preheat the oven to 375° and cook for an hour in a bain-marie.

Cool, unmold and refrigerate.

Serve with the whipped cream mixed with the remaining chiselled mint leaves.

Instead of monkfish, use any firm fleshed fish such as sea bass, striped bass, snapper, or halibut. If using the original in the recipe, the monkfish (lotte), remember to ask your fish seller to remove the skin, as it is tough and ugly.

Terrine de poissons aux herbes
Fish terrine with herbs

For six persons :
- ½ *pound of fresh salmon,*
- ½ *pound of whiting or seatrout fillets,*
- ½ *pound of chopped frozen spinach,*
- *3 eggs,*
- *3 egg whites,*
- *1 tablespoon of fresh chopped chives,*
- *1 tablespoon of chiseled tarragon,*
- *1 tablespoon of chopped parsley,*
- *1-2 stems of fresh fennel,*
- *1 ½ cups of heavy cream,*
- *6 slices of white bread,*
- *3 quarts of fish stock (see recipe p. 74),*
- *salt and pepper.*

Bring the fish stock to a boil in a deep kettle, then lower the flame, add the fish and simmer for no longer than five minutes.

Remove them with a slotted spoon, keeping the salmon and the whiting separate.

Cook the spinach in a saucepan until all of the water has evaporated.

Put the salmon through a food mill or food processor. Add an egg white, salt, pepper, the heavy cream, adding a little at a time until all of the ingredients form a smooth purée. Set aside.

Prepare the fillets of whiting or sea trout the same way and set aside.

Then, repeat again with the spinach. Set aside.

Make a stuffing with the crumbled bread, the three raw eggs, the tarragon, chives and parsley. Add salt and pepper and the remaining heavy cream. Mix well.

Butter a deep baking dish. Layer successively :
— the fennel stems
— the whiting purée

112

— the spinach purée
— the salmon purée
— the stuffing of bread, eggs and herbs.

Continue layering until you have used all of the variations.

Preheat the oven to 350°, and cook the terrine in a bain-marie for approximately 1 ½ hours.

Unmold. Serve hot with a beurre blanc, or cold with a green salad.

Sauces

Aïoli

For six persons :
- *12 cloves of garlic,*
- *2 egg yolks,*
- *1 pint of olive oil, or ½ pint of olive and ½ pint of peanut oil,*
- *1 pinch of salt,*
- *1 pinch of pepper,*
- *(juice of 1 lemon).*

Peel the garlic cloves and crush them thoroughly in a mortar. Place them into a mixing bowl, add the egg yolks, the salt and pepper, and mix well with a wooden spoon.

Continue stirring the egg/garlic mixture with one hand, while with the other, pour in a dripping flow of oil.

The sauce should become thicker and thicker, and the flow of oil may become faster. Never allow the sauce to become thin. When you have used all the oil and the desired consistency is achieved, you may add the juice of ½ a lemon. Salt and pepper. Keep refrigerated.

You may serve this sauce with boiled vegetables, cooked « al dente », such as carrots, turnips, potatoes, cauliflowers, chickpeas, etc. Also boiled salted cod, snails, and hard-boiled eggs.

Aïoli is the true essence of Provence and has become the symbol of that region of France.

In Provence, we use a mortar and a pestle to crush most of our ingredients. The mortar is a large heavy container made of marble, wood or stone. The pestle is made of the same materials. They should never be washed with soap, only rinsed with water and lemon or salt and vinegar.

Sauce au beurre d'anchois
Anchovy sauce

For six persons :
- *24 fillets of unsalted anchovies,*
- *$\frac{1}{2}$ pound of butter,*
- *2 tablespoons of olive oil,*
- *1 tablespoon of flour,*
- *2 tarragon sprigs or a teaspoon of dry tarragon.*

Wash the anchovies under a cold faucet for about 5 minutes. Place them in a mortar and mash them with a pestle, adding the olive oil very slowly. Process them through a food mill or a mixer.

Melt the butter in a small saucepan. Spinkle the flour in and stir constantly until golden, on very low fire. Stir in the mashed anchovies, one teaspoon at a time. Remove from the fire when you have a smooth paste.

Then add the tarragon, finely chiseled.

This sauce may be served with meat as well as with grilled fish .

Sauce tomate (chaude)
Tomato sauce (hot)

For six persons :
- *2 pounds of tomatoes,*
- *2 cloves of garlic,*
- *2 cloves ,*
- *1 pinch of thyme,*
- *2 bay leaves,*
- *1 pinch or 1 sprig of savory,*
- *2 tablespoons of chopped fresh basil,*
- *olive oil,*
- *salt and pepper*

Seed and coarsely chop the tomatoes, (or use a can of peeled whole stewing tomatoes).

In a deep skillet, heat 4 tablespoons of olive oil, the two cloves of crushed garlic, the thyme, the bay leaves, crumbled, the savory, the cloves and the basil. Then add the tomatoes and the salt and pepper.

Simmer very slowly with the lid on for 50 minutes minimum.

If you desire a heavier sauce, purée the tomatoes through a mixer, and heat them with 4 tablespoons of olive oil. Simmer and reduce the sauce until it becomes a paste.

Sauce provençale froide
Cold provençal sauce

For six persons :
- *2 cloves of garlic,*
- *3 fillets of anchovies, unsalted,*
- *2 egg yolks,*
- *1 lemon,*
- *5 tablespoons of olive oil,*
- *1 tablespoon of cold water,*
- *salt.*

In a mortar, mash the peeled garlic cloves and the anchovy fillets very thoroughly.

Add the two egg yolks, the cold water, a pinch of salt. Stir all and little by little, pour in the cup of olive oil. Then stir in the juice of the lemon.

This sauce should be light. It is perfect for grilled or cold meats and all fish.

Sauce aux poivrons
Red pepper sauce

For six persons :
- *2 red peppers,*
- *2 tomatoes,*
- *1 strong bird pimento or chili,*
- *¼ pound of ground almonds,*
- *1 cup of olive oil,*
- *salt and pepper.*

Preheat oven to 450°. Roast the tomatoes as they are. Cool, then peel and seed them.

Roast the peppers the same way, but seed them before.

Using a food processor or a food mill, mix the tomatoes, the peppers, the chili or bird pimento, and the almonds.

When the mixture is smooth, gradually add the oil as in a mayonnaise. Add salt and pepper.

This sauce, slightly hot, is perfect with all poached or grilled fish.

Tapenado
Tapenado sauce

For six persons :
- ½ *pound of pitted black olives,*
- ¼ *pound of unsalted anchovy fillets,*
- ¼ *cup of capers,*
- *5, tablespoons of olive oil,*
- *1 lemon,*
- *(1 tablespoon hot mustard),*
- *pepper.*

Into a food processor or a food mill, place the pitted olives, the anchovies and the capers. Mix well. Add the olive oil and the juice of the lemon. Pepper.

The tapenado is usually served on toasted bread for the « apéritif » or as a sauce for tender, raw young vegetables.

At the last moment, you may add a tablespoon of hot mustard, with thyme and a crumbled bay leaf.

Rouille

For six persons : • *3 cloves of garlic,*
• *2 red jalepeno peppers,*
• *2 slices of white bread,*
• *1 cup of milk,*
• *4 tablespoons of olive oil,*
• *3 tablespoons of fish stock,*
• *for second method - 1 egg yolk.*

There are two ways to prepare the "rouille".

First way : Crush the garlic cloves and the pimentoes in a mortar.

Soak the bread in the milk for a few minutes, drain and add to the mortar and crush again. Add the 4 tablespoons of olive oil. Continue to crush to obtain a smooth paste. Then incorporate the 3 tablespoons of fish stock.

Beware ! This is a very hot sauce.

Second way : You do not need the bread. You crush the garlic and the pimentoes, and make a mayonnaise with the egg yolk and the olive oil.

The second way is the most often used.

This sauce is used for all fish soups, especially bouillabaise. It is served on the side. Each guest stirs it into the soup, according to his taste.

Beurre de Montpellier
Montpellier butter

For six persons :
- *1 small bunch of fresh tarragon,*
- *1 small bunch of parsley,*
- *1 small bunch of chives,*
- *¼ pound of fresh spinach,*
- *1 bunch of watercress,*
- *1 tablespoon of capers,*
- *3 anchovy fillets,*
- *2 shallots,*
- *2 eggs,*
- *1 clove of garlic,*
- *¼ pound of butter,*
- *5 tablespoons of olive oil,*
- *2 small sour gherkins (cornichons),*
- *salt and pepper.*

Blanch the tarragon, the parsley, the chives, the watercress, the spinach, and the shallots in boiling water for 3 minutes. Drain and rinse under cold water, then drain thoroughly.

Plunge the eggs in boiling water for 8-10 minutes. Remove and put them in cold water for about 3 minutes. Then peel. Set aside only the yolks.

Put all of the herbs into a mortar or a food processor with the finely chopped gherkins. Then add the anchovies, the capers and the garlic clove. Crush or mix until you obtain a smooth paste. Correct seasoning with salt and pepper. Add the egg yolks and the butter.

When the mixture is a very smooth purée, pass it through a sieve (if using a food processor, this step is not necessary).

Rinse the mortar. Put back the purée and gradually add the olive oil, mixing thoroughly. It should become very thick. Taste and correct seasoning if needed.

This sauce is perfect with fish, poached or grilled.

Fromage blanc aux herbes fines
Cottage cheese with herbs

For six persons :
- *½ pint of cottage cheese,*
- *1 cup of sour cream,*
- *1 cup of heavy cream,*
- *2 tablespoons of chopped parsley,*
- *1 tablespoon of chervil, chopped,*
- *1 tablespoon of tarragon, chiseled,*
- *1 tablespoon of chives, minced,*
- *1 tablespoon of fresh mint, chiseled,*
- *5 tablespoons of olive oil,*
- *1 tablespoon of white vinegar,*
- *salt and pepper.*

Whisk the sour cream, the cottage cheese, and heavy cream together with the oil and the vinegar, or mix it with a food processor. Add salt and pepper.

Stir in all the herbs, taste and correct seasoning.

Refrigerate and serve very cold with raw vegetables such as carrots, cucumbers, endives, celery, etc.

In America, you may use small curd cottage cheese and mix it with sour cream.

Sauce fenouil
Fennel sauce

For six persons :
- *1 bunch of fresh fennel,*
- *1 cup of olive oil,*
- *2 tablespoons of fresh tomato sauce,*
- *1 pinch of flour,*
- *1 pinch of nutmeg,*
- *salt and pepper*

Blanch the fennel in salted boiling water for 10 minutes. Cool and drain. Chop it finely.

Heat the olive oil in a skillet. Add one tablespoon of the tomato sauce, and half of the chopped fennel. Stir with a wooden spoon. Salt and pepper to taste.

Sprinkle with the flour. When it becomes golden, add the rest of the tomato sauce and the fennel, with the pinch of nutmeg.

Stir and simmer, uncovered, for 10 minutes.

This sauce is excellent with all fish, poached or grilled.

Cheese

Boumian

- *4-6 hard goat cheeses (Crotins or Pélardons),*
- *1 quart of olive oil,*
- *1 quart of dry white wine,*
- *4-5 cloves of garlic,*
- *1 tablespoon of dry herbs (thyme, etc...),*
- *1 tablespoon of brandy (Armagnac, if possible)*

Pour the olive oil and the wine into a glass jar. Add the cheeses in layers.

Add the garlic cloves, the herbs and the brandy.

Let stand for 48 hours. The cheeses should become softer.

I recommend a good red Côte du Rhône, such as Châteauneuf, with these cheeses.

Hard goat cheese is rather difficult to find in America. You may substitute a cheese called « Banon », or use 2-3 Montrachets and let them marinate for 24 hours.

Bocal de fromages de chèvre à l'huile d'olive
Goat cheeses preserved in olive oil

For one glass jar, 2 quarts size, with a wide opening :

- *30 small goat cheeses, fresh,*
- *2 minced shallots,*
- *2-3 cloves of garlic,*
- *14 black peppercorns,*
- *2 sprigs of thyme,*
- *4 bay leaves,*
- *1 quart of olive oil,*
- *½ sweet red pepper, grilled and sliced,*
- *3 sprigs of tarragon,*
- *1 branch of rosemary,*
- *1 small bunch of parsley.*

Line the bottom of the jar with 3-4 goat cheeses, several peppercorns, thyme, shallots, bay leaves, a garlic clove, a sprig of parsley and some rosemary.

Repeat this process with the cheeses and the spices until the jar is full. Do not crowd them. Pour in the olive oil. Close the jar and let the cheeses rest in the fragrant olive oil for at least one month.

Serve with a chilled rosé wine.

This delicacy should keep for at least one month.

Desserts

Pommes au four
Baked apples

For six persons : • *6 large apples, (Golden or Granny Smith),*
• *¼ pound of butter,*
• *¼ cup of sugar,*
• *1 teaspoon of vanilla,*
• *1 glass of water*

Peel the apples, and remove the cores, taking some of the pulp with it.

Mash the pulp. Add the softened butter, the vanilla and the sugar.

Fill the apples with this purée.

Place them on a shallow baking dish, and bake for approximately one hour at 325°. Moisten them with water from time to time.

Serve hot.

Melon de Cavaillon au vin d'orange
Cantaloup with orange wine

For four persons : • *1 large ripe cantaloup,*
• *3 tablespoons of sugar,*
• *1 cup of orange wine (see recipe p. 138)*

Cut, seed and peel the cantaloup. Dice the flesh.

In a mixing bowl, sprinkle the melon with sugar and pour the orange wine over it.

Refrigerate for at least 2 hours.

Serve very cold in glass cups.

Salade de fruits frais
Fresh fruit salad

For six persons :
- *2 pears,*
- *2 peaches,*
- *2 apricots,*
- *¼ pound of strawberries,*
- *1 large tablespoon of golden raisins,*
- *1 small ripe cantaloup,*
- *1 wedge of watermelon,*
- *½ cup of pear brandy (alcool de poire, Manguin or Williams),*
- *½ cup of sugar.*

Peel and dice all the fruits.

In a large bowl, sprinkle them with sugar and moisten with the pear brandy. Refrigerate for 2 hours.

Serve very cold.

Compote de fruits
Fruit compote

For six persons :
- *3 pears,*
- *3 peaches,*
- *3 apples,*
- *3 apricots,*
- *1 vanilla bean,*
- *¼ cup of sugar,*
- *1 cup of water.*

Peel the fruits and quarter them. Place them in a heavy enamel casserole. Add the water, the sugar and the vanilla bean.

Simmer for 20 minutes.

Serve hot or cold.

133

Fraises au citron
Strawberries with lemon

For four persons : • *1 ½ pints of strawberries,*
• *3 lemons,*
• *½ cup of sugar,*
• *1 teaspoon of vanilla.*

Wash and hull the strawberries.

In a deep serving bowl, arrange one pint of the strawberries.

Purée the rest of the strawberries in a food processor, adding the lemon juice, the sugar and the vanilla.

Pour over the strawberries, refrigerate and serve very cold.

Poires au vin
Pears in wine

For six persons : • *6 large pears,*
• *1 quart of good red wine,*
• *1 cinnamon stick,*
• *1 vanilla bean,*
• *½ cup of sugar,*
• *1 teaspoon of vanilla.*

Peel the pears, leave whole and leave the stem.

Pour the red wine into an enamel casserole. Add the pears, the vanilla, the cinnamon, and the sugar.

Simmer for 40 minutes. Let cool. Serve cold, with the mulled wine.

Sorbet à la pêche
Peach sherbet

For six persons : • *6 large peaches,*
• *1 cup of sugar,*
• *1 cup of water,*
• *2 lemons,*
• *½ cup of peach brandy.*

Boil the water and the sugar in a heavy saucepan. Remove when it becomes syrupy. Let cool.

Peel the peaches and remove the pits. Purée through a food processor. You should have a light, runny purée. Add the lemon juice, the cooled syrup, stir thoroughly.

Pour into an ice maker and freeze for at least 3 hours.

One hour before serving, remove the sherbet from the freezer and put into the refrigerator to soften it.

Serve in glasses, moistened with peach brandy.

Les treize desserts
The thirteen Christmas desserts

These are the original provençal desserts, the thirteen of them, the way they were served long, long, ago :

Raisins - Dry figs - Almonds - Walnuts - Hazelnuts, these are called « mendiants », meaning beggars - Pears - Apples - Plums - Nougat noir -

Nougat blanc (Nougats are sweets/pastes made with syrup/honey/walnuts/hazelnuts. They are traditional in the north of Provence. Montelimar is the town famous for its « nougats ») - Fougasse, or pompe à huile (sort of brioche made with oil) - Quince jam - Watermelon jam.

But today the traditions have become less strict and everyone adds to this theme his own variations. So we find : oranges, dates, tangerines, honeydew melons, oreillettes (the recipe follows), calissons d'Aix (almond paste with hazelnuts and pistachios), papillottes, etc.

137

Vin d'orange
Orange wine

In Provence, old customs are faithfully followed, particulary for Christmas and Twelfth Night Celebration.

Orange wine is a must with the traditional Christmas « Pompe à l'huile » (see recipe p. 139) and with the very popular Twelfth Night cake (see recipe p. 140).

For 1 quart of orange wine :
- *1 bitter or Seville orange,*
- *½ sweet orange,*
- *1 quart of rosé or white wine,*
- *5 tablespoons of good brandy (Armagnac is best),*
- *½ pound of sugar,*
- *5 tablespoons of quinquina wine.*

Use only the thin skins of the oranges.

Mix all the ingredients, cover and let stand for approximately one month.

When ready, filter.

Drink it for Christmas. You may also drink it, however, in the summertime as a very cold "aperitif".

Pompe à huile (ou fougasse)

For ten to twelve persons :
- *2 pounds of flour, unbleached,*
- *¾ pound of sugar,*
- *1 cup of olive oil,*
- *1 pinch of salt,*
- *½ cup of orange blossom water,*
- *5 tablespoons of water.*

The day before, mix the flour and the water in a mixing bowl. Cover the bowl, place in a warm corner, such as the top of the stove, and let stand overnight.

The next day, knead together this paste with the remaining flour, the olive oil and the orange blossom water. Add the salt.

Make a ball, place it in a mixing bowl, cover it with several thick towels and let stand for 2 hours in a warm place.

The dough will have doubled in size.

Roll out the dough to form a circle and place it on a slightly oiled baking sheet. With a sharp knife, draw a deep crisscross or another design of your choice.

Preheat oven at 375° and bake for 25 minutes.

This cake, only made for Christmas, is a provençal tradition.

Gâteau des rois
Twelfth night cake

This cake is a joyful occasion for family reunions which may last through January until the beginning of February.

For 6 persons : • *2 pounds of flour,*
  • *¾ pound of sugar,*
  • *1 lemon peel, grated,*
  • *6 eggs,*
  • *1 egg (beaten),*
  • *½ pound of butter,*
  • *½ pound of candied fruits,*
  • *18 lumps of sugar, coarsely pounded,*
  • *1 teaspoon of baking powder,*
  • *1 dry bean.*

Take ½ pound of flour and make a dough with the baking powder and the lukewarm water.

With the rest of the flour, make a well. Put into it the 3/4 pound of sugar, the lemon peel and 3 eggs.

Knead this dough briskly, adding 3 more eggs, one by one.

Incorporate the first dough, and work it well until it stops sticking to the fingers and the table.

Still kneading the dough, add the butter by small pieces, and half of the candied fruits.

Mould the dough in a crownlike shape. Put it on a flat baking sheet which you will have buttered and dredged with flour.

Let it rise sufficiently. Press a finger on it, release it, if the dough comes back to its original shape, it is ready to be cooked.

Brush the cake with the beaten egg, slip the dry bean into it, and bake in a slow oven.

When cooked, decorate with the rest of the candied fruits and the pounded sugar.

Be sure not to forget the dry bean as the person who will discover it will become king/queen of the evening.

Oreillettes

For six persons :
- *1 pound of flour,*
- *¼ cup of sugar,*
- *3 eggs,*
- *1 lemon peel,*
- *1 orange peel,*
- *¼ cup of orange flower water,*
- *2 tablespoons of butter,*
- *1 pinch of salt,*
- *1 cup of oil for frying.*

Shred the lemon and orange peels through a grater.

Mix them with the flour, the softened butter, the sugar, the orange water and the three eggs, already beaten. Add the pinch of salt.

Knead the dough, adding a little water if necessary. Let stand, covered, for 2 hours.

Place the dough on a lightly floured board or marble and roll it out with a rolling pin. Then, using a pastry wheele or a very sharp knife, cut the dough in squares of about 4 inches.

Heat the oil in a deep frying pan, and when very hot, fry the « oreillettes ».

When they are golden, remove and drain them on paper towels. Sprinkle with confectioner's sugar.

Cool summer drinks

Aigre-doux
Bittersweet

For six average glasses : • *1 quart of strawberries,*
• *4 lemons,*
• *club soda.*

In a pitcher, mix crushed ice, the juice of 4 lemons and the juice of 1 quart of strawberries (simply pass them through a food processor).

Add club soda, or seltzer.

Decorate the drink with one orange slice, a lemon peel and a strawberry.

Drink very cold.

Jus de tomate
Tomato juice

For six average glasses : • *1 quart of tomato juice,*
• *12 sprigs of fresh mint.*

Pour the juice into a pitcher.

Crush the mint in a mortar.

Add the mint to the juice. Place in the refrigerator and let macerate for 3 hours.

Serve ice cold, decorated with mint leaves. If you desire a stronger drink, add a jigger of gin to each glass and stir.

Cocktail de fruits
Fruit cocktail

In a large pitcher, mix the following proportions :

- *1/3 of fresh pineapple pulp,*
- *1/3 of fresh orange juice,*
- *1/3 of fresh lemon juice.*

Stir well. Refrigerate for 4 hours. Serve with fresh mint leaves.

Café glacé à la menthe
Iced coffee with mint

For six average glasses :
- *1 quart of hot water,*
- *12 teaspoons of instant coffee,*
- *6 teaspoons of sugar,*
- *20 fresh mint leaves,*
- *2 teaspoons of white "crème de menthe".*

In a large pitcher, mix the coffee, the sugar and the "crème de menthe". Fill with ice cubes and pour in the hot water.

Add the mint leaves. Refrigerate for 4 hours.

When serving do not remove the leaves, as they will continue to impart flavor in the coffee as long as they are in it.

Méli-mélo

In a large shaker, mix :

- *3/5 of tomato juice,*
- *1/5 of fresh orange juice,*
- *1/5 of fresh lemon juice.*

Add crusched ice. Shake well and serve in iced glasses.

Infusion de verveine glacée
Verbena infusion on ice

For six average glasses : • *1 quart of water,*
- *10-12 fresh verbena sprigs,*
- *2 sprigs of fresh mint,*
- *3 lemons.*

Boil the water and brew the verbena and the mint for at least three hours.

When cool, add the juice of the three lemons.

Store all day in the refrigerator.

Pour over ice. Sugar may be added.

Tilleul au cassis
Infusion of linden leaves with black currant

For six average glasses : • *1 quart of water,*
• *2 tablespoons of linden leaves,*
• *2 tablespoons of black currant syrup.*

Brew the linden leaves in boiling water and let stand for 45 minutes.

Stir in the black currant syrup. Pour over ice.

Serve very cold.

Citronnade
Lemonade

For six average glasses : • *1 quart of water,*
• *2 lemons,*
• *10 teaspoons of sugar.*

Cut the lemons in into thin slices and place them in a pitcher. Pour the boiling water and the sugar over them.

Drain and let cool.

Cover, refrigerate and serve on ice with lemon wedges.

Living in Provence

Dîner à deux
Dinner for two

Leek cake

Grilled bass with fennel sauce

White rice, sautéed in olive oil

Fresh fruit salad

Dans la cuisine, pour les amis
Dinner for friends, in the kitchen

Spring lamb from the Alpilles, braised with thyme

Zucchini provençal

Chicory with garlic dressing

Fresh fruit compote

Un déjeuner simple
A simple lunch

Basil custard

Calf liver provençal

Browned hearts of artichokes

Goat cheeses

Strawberries with lemon

L'apéritif chez Papou
Cocktail at Papou's

Pastis

Kir

Black olives with thyme

Salami from Arles

Toasts with tapenado

Cottage cheese with herbs

Little stick of raw vegetables from the garden
(celery, cucumbers, carrots)

Papou is the nickname of Régine Deméry. She is part of our Souleiado clan, as a matter of fact she is the warm, tender heart of it.

Pique-nique dans les Alpilles
Picnic in the hills

Small provençal patés with herbs

Vegetable terrine

Salad with tapenado

Grilled pork chops with sage

Goat cheeses : Crottins, Pelardons, Banons, etc.

Basket of fresh fruits

Soirée gitane
A gypsy evening

Crespeou

"Gardianne" Salad

Skewered beef with a herb butter sauce

Goat cheese in olive oil

Cantaloup with orange wine

Sous la tonnelle
Under the trees

Pink stucco, green shutters,

and

Pistou...

Green salad

Goat cheese in olive oil

Fresh fruits

Couleurs d'automne
Shades of autumn

Mushroom terrine

Stew of baby squids

Bohémienne

Baked Apples

C'est l'hiver
Winter has come...

Provençal pie

Lamb shoulder with lima beans

Green salad

Pears in wine

Soir de fête
Celebration !

Fish terrine with herbs

White wine of Châteauneuf-du-Pape

Leg of lamb with cream of garlic

Grilled tomatoes "à la provençale"

Crunchy balls of eggplants

Red wine of Châteauneuf-du-Pape

Peach sherbet and almond tiles

Peach brandy « Manguin »

Lendemain de fête
The day after the celebration

Aïgo boulido

Mes bonnes adresses en Provence
My favorite places in Provence

There is no good cuisine without the best ingredients. I find mine in the open markets of Provence :
Arles, on saturday morning, (the wonderful, famous market of Arles)
Tarascon, on tuesday
Saint-Rémy, on wednesday.
I buy my olive oil from the mill in Maussane-les-Alpilles, at the foot of the Baux valley.
The craked olives are from Mouriès.
I choose my wine in the cooperative cellars of Tavel, Lirac and Châteauneuf-du-Pape.
Peach and pear brandy are from Manguin.
Ceramic dishes and utensils are made in Uzès, at Pichon.

My favorite restaurants are :

« Le café des arts » at Silvio's in Saint-Rémy.
« Ou ravi provençau » at Aurore and Jean François, in Maussane
« Le mas Teulière » at Christou's on the road to Saint-Rémy, in Maussane.
And « Au Paradou » at René Quenin for the pastis under the sycamores.

All my warm thanks to :

_ Jean Pierre Deméry, owe him the idea of this book.
_ Monsieur Frédéric Dard who honored me with his preface.
_ Jerry Hartley for his drawings.
_ Nicole and Madeleine, our faithful friends in Paradou.
_ Régine and Christine Deméry who so sweetly and gracefully open their houses to me.
_ To the photographers : Jacques Primois, Michel Holsnyder, Michaël Dunne, M. Daspet.
_ and to my publishers, les Editions Rivages, who trusted me.

Index

Meat and poultry

Patés and terrines

6e édition